SOUTH WEST COAST PATH
Falmouth to Exmouth

SOUTH WEST COAST PATH

Falmouth to Exmouth

Brian Le Messurier

Photographs by Mike Williams
General editor Michael Allaby

AURUM PRESS

COUNTRYSIDE COMMISSION · ORDNANCE SURVEY

ACKNOWLEDGEMENTS

The opportunity to write this guide seemed particularly apposite. Both my mother and grandfather were born at St Anthony Lighthouse at the west end of this stretch of the Coast Path. I work for the National Trust producing publications about its coastal properties in Devon and Cornwall, and live in Exeter, which sits astride the Exe, the eastern terminus of that section of the Coast Path covered by this book.

Ten years ago I wrote the first-generation official guide book to the *South Devon Coast Path*, but that book, and the series of which it was a part, is vastly out of date, so a new, consumer-orientated set of guide books was necessary for the many more people who now walk the Coast Path.

I am grateful to the following for assistance: the staff of the National Trust in Devon and Cornwall, the officers of the South Devon and South Cornwall Heritage Coast Services, the several kind friends who ferried me back to the start of my walking stints, and the others who provided companionship along the way and that vital second car on the longer sections.

This edition first published 1990 by Aurum Press Ltd in association
with the Countryside Commission and the Ordnance Survey
Text copyright © 1990 by Aurum Press Ltd, the Countryside
Commission and the Ordnance Survey
Maps Crown copyright © 1990 by the Ordnance Survey
Photographs copyright © 1990 by the Countryside Commission

British Library Cataloguing in Publication Data

Le Messurier, Brian
South West Coast Path: Falmouth to Exmouth.
– (National trail guides; 10)
1. South-west England. Coastal regions. Long-distance
footpaths: South-west peninsula Coast Path.
Recreations: Walking. Visitors' guides
I. Title   II. Allaby, Michael 1933–   III. Series
769.5'09423

ISBN 1 85410 096 3
OS ISBN 0 319 00197 0

Book design by Robert Updegraff
Cover photograph: north-west from Rame Head to Plymouth Sound
Title page photograph: John Campbell's houses on Chapel Point, Mevagissey.

Typeset by Wyvern Typesetting Ltd, Bristol
Printed and bound in Italy by Printers Srl, Trento

Contents

Circular walks appear on pages 32, 48, 80, 92, 104 and 126

How to use this guide

The 594-mile (956-kilometre) South West Coast Path is covered by four national trail guides. This book describes the Coast Path from Falmouth to Exmouth, 172 miles (277 kilometres). Companion guides describe the Coast Path from Minehead to Padstow, from Padstow to Falmouth, and from Exmouth to Poole. Each guide therefore covers a section of the Coast Path between major estuaries, where walkers may need a ferry or other transport.

This guide is in three parts:

• The introduction, historical background to the area and advice for walkers.

• The Coast Path itself, described in eleven chapters, with maps opposite each route description. This part of the guide also includes information on places of interest as well as six circular walks spaced out along the Path, three in the Cornish section, and three in Devon, starting either from the Coast Path or at an inland car park. Key sites are numbered in the text and on the maps to make it easy to follow the route description.

• The last part includes useful information, such as local transport, ferries and river crossings, accommodation, organisations involved with the Coast Path, and further reading.

The maps have been prepared by the Ordnance Survey using 1:25 000 Pathfinder or Outdoor Leisure maps as a base. The line of the Coast Path is shown in yellow, with the status of each section of the Coast Path – footpath or bridleway for example – shown in green underneath (see key on inside front cover). These rights of way markings also indicate the precise alignment of the Coast Path, which walkers should follow. In some cases the yellow line on these maps may show a route which is different from that shown on older maps. Walkers are then recommended to follow the yellow route in this guide, which is that waymarked with the distinctive acorn symbol 🌰 used for all national trails. Any parts of the Coast Path that may be difficult to follow on the ground are clearly highlighted in the route description, and important points to watch for are marked with letters in each chapter, both in the text and on the maps. *Black arrows (➤) at the edge of the maps indicate the start point.* Should there have been a need to alter the route since the publication of this guide, walkers are advised to follow the signs which have been erected on site to indicate this.

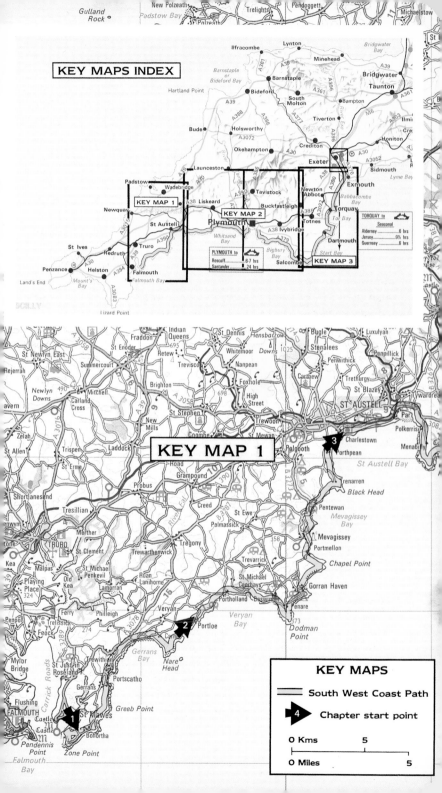

KEY MAP 2

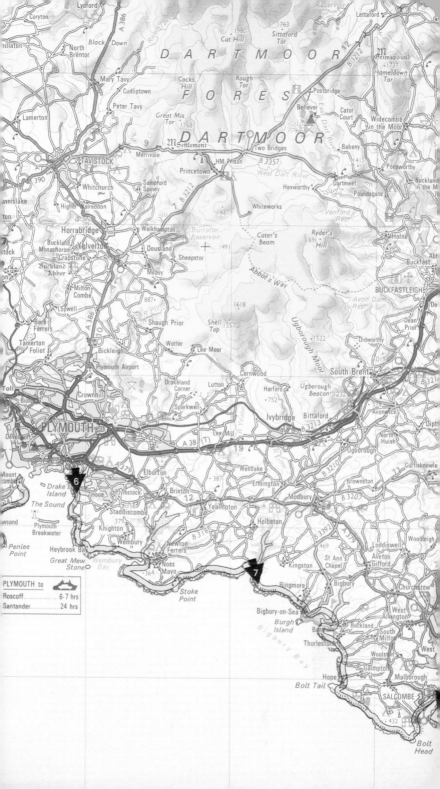

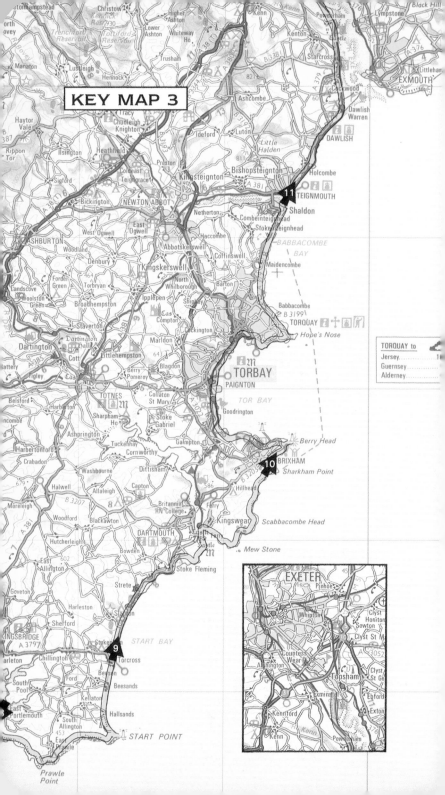

Distance checklist

This list will assist you in calculating the distances between places on the Coast Path where you may be planning to stay overnight, or in checking your progress along the way.

location	approx. distance from previous location	
	miles	km
Place (south side of Percuil River – no ferry)	0	0
Portscatho	6.0	9.7
Portloe	7.2	11.6
Gorran Haven	8.4	13.5
Mevagissey	3.3	5.3
Charlestown	7.0	11.3
Polkerris	5.3	8.5
Fowey (Fowey Harbour – west)	4.4	7.1
Polruan (Fowey Harbour – east)	0	0
Polperro	6.8	10.9
Looe (bridge joining East and West Looe)	4.9	7.9
Portwrinkle	7.5	12.1
Kingsand/Cawsand	9.9	15.9
Cremyll (west side of ferry across Tamar)	3.2	5.1
Turnchapel (south side of Cattewater)	0	0
Warren Point (Wembury) (Yealm Estuary – west)	6.8	10.9
Noss Mayo (Yealm Estuary – east)	0	0
Mothecombe (Erme Estuary – west)	8.3	13.4
Wonwell (Erme Estuary – east)	0.4	0.6
Cockleridge (Avon Estuary – west)	5.8	9.3
Bantham (Avon Estuary – east)	0	0
Salcombe (Salcombe Harbour – west)	12.2	19.6
East Portlemouth (Salcombe Harbour – east)	0	0
Torcross	12.7	20.4
Dartmouth (Dartmouth Harbour – west)	10.1	16.3
Kingswear (Dartmouth Harbour – east)	0	0
Brixham	11.0	17.7
Torquay Harbour	8.3	13.4
Shaldon (Teign Estuary – south)	10.8	17.4
Teignmouth (Teign Estuary – north)	0	0
Starcross (Exe Estuary – west)	7.6	12.2
Topsham Lock (west side of Topsham foot ferry)	4.2	6.8

Preface

The South West Coast Path is one of the national trails in England and Wales that the Countryside Commission promotes for walkers – and, in the case of some trails, for riders – to explore and enjoy the best of our countryside, far away from towns, traffic and the bustle of urban life.

These trails are particularly suited for long journeys, but they can also be sampled on an afternoon or over a weekend. Another way of using them is as part of a round trip, or circular walk, and suggestions for these are included in this guide. National trails are maintained by local or national park authorities on behalf of the Commission, and are well waymarked with our distinctive acorn. Each trail provides an enjoyable, and sometimes challenging, walk or ride in the countryside.

National trails run through the grandest and most beautiful countryside and coast which England and Wales have to offer. Many of them also link with other waymarked paths, thus making it possible to plan a variety of journeys throughout the countryside.

Although the length of the South West Coast Path was previously cited as 515 miles, the measurements given in these guide books are the actual distances walked, including sections through towns and villages, which total 594 miles (956 km).

We hope you will enjoy walking along the South West Coast Path and that this guide to the section between Falmouth and Exmouth will help to make your journey one to remember.

Sir Derek Barber
Chairman
Countryside Commission

PART ONE

INTRODUCTION

The landscape along the Coast Path

This stretch of the English coast has enormous variety, ranging from the soaring cliff tops of Bolberry Down and the Dodman to the fen-like estuary margins of the River Exe; from cosy Cornish coves to the spacious sweep of Slapton Sands; and from tiny fishing villages, such as Portloe and Polkerris, to the teeming population of Plymouth.

A great deal of the landscape has been granted official designation, generally for protective reasons. Heritage coasts are described later in the book. The South Cornwall Heritage Coast extends from the Fal to Plymouth, and the South Devon Heritage Coast from Wembury Beach to Sharkham Point (Brixham). Other sections of the route are designated as sites of special scientific interest (SSSIs) and areas of outstanding natural beauty (AONBs).

Extensive lengths of the coast are owned by the National Trust, and these include large areas of agricultural land. The public has no access over these fields which are farmed by the Trust's tenants. However, many link paths have been provided by the Trust across the intervening fields, and often these connect to small car parks, thus making it possible to work out circular walks.

A glance at the map of South West England will show that the headlands of the Lizard, Prawle Point/Start Point and Portland Bill project southwards from the roughly west-to-east land mass of Cornwall, Devon and Dorset. But once walking the Coast Path these national features seem less important, and the decisive headlands are promontories such as Nare Head, the Dodman, Rame Head, Berry Head and Hope's Nose. Between these jutting cliffs there are lesser protrusions, such as Black Head and Bolt Tail.

As you move along the Coast Path, keep your eye open for the human features that enliven the coastline, and seem to add, rather than detract, from the scene. For instance, the 19th century Daymarks on the Gribbin and near Coleton Fishacre have an architectural distinction which one doubts could be repeated today. Terraces of coastguard cottages – there are

The ruined, but partly restored, church of St Peter the Poor Fisherman, near Noss Mayo in Devon.

some to be seen at Portloe, Cawsand and above Cellars Beach at the mouth of the Yealm – speak of the government's fight against smuggling.

In some villages with a history of fishing, particularly in Cornwall, it is worth looking out for the high stone walls of the old pilchard cellars or 'palaces'. These were fish factories where pilchards were prepared for the home market, or for export. There are some fine examples at Portwrinkle and Kingsand – along the beach to the north of the village.

Massive lime kilns speak of efforts to improve the soil in the days before artificial fertilisers. There are sources of limestone at Torbay and Plymouth, so from these places small vessels brought the limestone to be burnt, and coal was delivered by sea from South Wales. There was a great deal of commercial boat activity in the 18th and 19th centuries.

Archaeological remains are less easy to spot, but are indicated in the route descriptions, and marked on the map. Forts and castles of every era from the Iron Age to the Second World War will be seen, and they cluster particularly round Plymouth, such an important naval base and anchorage.

Planning your walk

Only you, the walker, can decide when and how to walk this stretch of the Coast Path. There are many factors to take into account, not least the very practical matter of getting across the thirteen stretches of water that have to be tackled between leaving Falmouth and crossing the Exe. Obstacles they may be, but they provide entertaining interludes to your pedestrian progress.

However, the off-season walker may have good reason to rue their presence, as you must consider a lengthy diversion round the Rivers Yealm and Avon. You must be prepared to wade the Erme if you can time your arrival at the crossing point for the bottom of the ebb tide when the river is running low (i.e. no floodwater), or face a similar lengthy detour. Even reaching the start of this stretch of Coast Path at Place requires a taxi, a friend's car or a privately negotiated trip with a St Mawes' boatman if the walker is deterred from an 8-mile (13-km) walk along roads and paths via St Just-in-Roseland and Gerrans. Anyone travelling from east to west and arriving at Place slipway must not expect as much as a phone box to greet him. Full details of the estuary crossings, and the lack of them, are given on pages 157–60.

The seasonal ferries may limit the long-distance walker to the main holiday period, but this is perhaps the least attractive time to be on the Coast Path as so many other people are there as well, particularly in the more populated areas. The second half of May and early June are best for wild flowers and birds, June and July are probably the warmest months, and April and September can give days of extraordinarily clear visibility along the coast.

A fine day in winter can be a rewarding time to stroll beside Slapton Ley or the Exe Estuary, for then one can see birds which in summer are in the Arctic.

Bus services are infrequent or non-existent out of season, and refreshment points closed. Some lavatories are even bolted and barred, often because the water is turned off to prevent frost damage.

Accommodation must be considered, and good local advice taken. Tourist information centres (TICs), where this can be enquired about, are listed in the useful information section. Public transport details can be obtained from the addresses in the same section.

Equipment

If you are backpacking you will obviously have to carry everything, but the day walker or the person staying overnight in a 'b & b' can travel much lighter. Regardless of where you are planning to lay your head, a camera, a small pair of binoculars and a simple compass should be carried, and a waterproof is *de rigeur*, even in mid-summer. I strongly advocate carrying a towel and bathing gear near the top of one's kit: there are so many attractive coves to tempt one down. After a swim the wet things can be tied to the outside of a rucksack to dry.

As to what to wear, there is a danger of being over-dressed. I quite happily walked from Polruan to Polperro in mid-summer in training shoes, shorts and a T-shirt, but could have done with a floppy hat on that particular day to keep the sun out of my eyes. A woolly hat is comfortable in the winter, and acts like a tea cosy. I am a great believer in trainers so long as mud is not anticipated. The Coast Path is incredibly steep in places, and to lift up a pair of heavy boots several hundred times is exceedingly tiring. Shorts make for greater freedom of movement than trousers. The path is mostly well maintained, and the days of having to force a way through bramble thickets are long past.

One's mental equipment is as important as the gear on one's back, and I have found that, faced with a steep climb, it helps to put the brain into neutral, or at least think of something other than the matter in hand. Also, do not attempt too much in one day. Break up the route into easily attainable sections, and this will give opportunities to deviate from the Coast Path to look at features that catch the eye. The intention should be to enjoy each day as it happens, and not to be thinking of, say, the Exe Estuary on the day you leave the Fal. There are so many wonderful intermediate objectives that the final goal need not be considered for many days.

Finding your way

Route finding should not be a problem. After all, providing you keep the sea's location in mind you should pick up the path again without trouble. Occasional problems occur where there are alternative paths, but again, it does not really matter; you will get there in the end. Examples of high and low paths will be found to the west of Polperro, east of Salcombe, between Kingswear and Brixham, and north of Torquay, and there are others.

Perhaps the greatest difficulty in finding the way arises in a built-up area. For instance, knowing which narrow street to follow at Looe when walking eastwards can lead to some head-scratching.

If you are lost, do ask where you are. Better this than trespass on private land. Never take a short cut across cultivated fields or climb fences or hedges in the hope of reaching a road. This will do nothing for the reputation of walkers among the farming community.

A few places exist where it is likely there will be path changes during the currency of this guide, so walkers are urged to keep their eyes open and follow the signs and waymarks if they find information conflicting with this book, which gives the position as it was in 1988. Scope exists for improvement in the line of the Coast Path, and negotiations are constantly being undertaken to bring this about. Nothing is set in concrete or inscribed on tablets of stone. Be prepared for things to change.

Safety precautions

If you are careful you should not have cause to worry about your personal safety on the Coast Path, but it is well to remember that you are following the edge of the land, and chunks of cliff do crumble away from time to time.

After rain the steep slopes are very slippery, so do exercise care when the surfaces are wet. Good treads on your footwear may save a fall, and if you are walking solo a whistle will attract attention. A simple first-aid kit should also be carried.

Perhaps most of the risks will arise when you leave the Coast Path – to swim or sit on the beach. Local advice about bathing is well taken – coves are usually safe, but swimming off headlands is hazardous. Sitting beneath cliffs could lead to you being struck by falling rock, and if you venture round the shoreline into a neighbouring cove you could be cut off by a rising tide.

Lastly, the chance of getting sunburnt is very real on the coast, so cover up those sensitive parts, particularly the head and the back of the neck, if the skies are clear. This affliction has a habit of creeping up unnoticed and can totally spoil a holiday.

PART TWO

SOUTH WEST COAST PATH
Falmouth to Exmouth

1 Crossing the Fal, and on to Portloe

from Place via Portscatho
13¼ miles (21.3 km)

The problems on the Coast Path between the Fal and the Exe begin as soon as you reach St Mawes **1** via the year-round ferry from Falmouth. You are immediately thwarted in your desire to reach Place, the true commencement of this stretch of path. Ferries no longer ply their trade across the Percuil River, so you must make alternative arrangements.

While contemplating this next step it is worth taking a look at St Mawes, which is much more than a stepping stone on the Coast Path. Once a fishing village (with a pilotage speciality), like several dozen others on the Cornish coast, St Mawes has gone up-market in the last 80 years, and is now one of the county's premier yachting centres.

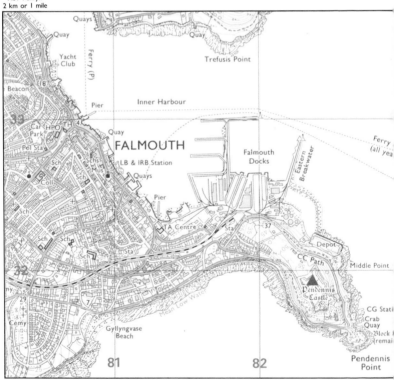

FALMOUTH BAY

A 10-minute walk to the west of the harbour is St Mawes Castle, a well-preserved fortification built by Henry VIII in 1538 when he began to look to the nation's coastal defences after his excommunication. The plan imitates a clover leaf, and the keep is mounted atop the trefoil. Across the water is Pendennis Castle, Henry's other castle in this area. St Mawes Castle is owned by English Heritage and is open at the times advertised.

The most obvious ploys to cross the Percuil River are to take a taxi from St Mawes to Place, or to engage the services of a boatman, and between Easter and the end of September there should be no difficulty on this score. Large parties of walkers may be able to charter a special ferry from Falmouth direct to Place (see ferry and river crossings section, page 158).

A walk around the creek heads of the Percuil River is a possibility, but will add at least 8 miles (13 km) to your journey, as well as a certain amount of roadwork, even if you proceed north from St Mawes along the west-facing cliff path to St Just-in-Roseland.

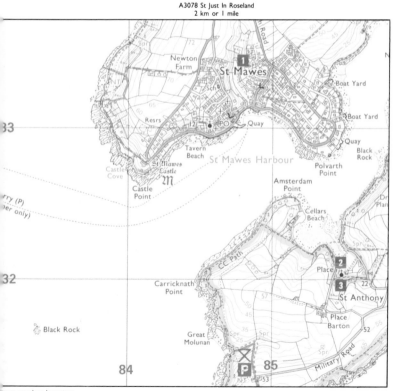

ours are given in metres
e vertical interval is 5m

If you are walking east-to-west to Place and want to cross to St Mawes you must not expect to find an obliging boatman prepared to act as ferryman, and there is not even a phone box from which to call a taxi. You should make plans for your onward progress before reaching the end of the Coast Path, and Portscatho or its neighbour Gerrans are the places to do this. A glance at the map may tempt the east-to-west walker to omit this remote headland south of Portscatho, but its very inaccessibility is one of its charms.

I will assume you have reached Place by whatever means. At high tide, the point of access is the slipway. At low tide, Totty's Steps was the landing for the ferry from St Mawes 1 and these are reached along the path on the east side of Place Creek, and a few yards inside Drawler Plantation.

The Ordnance Survey map shows a public right of way across the creek from the slipway, but if the tide is in, the 'path' is under water, and if the tide is out, the path – which does not exist on the ground – would be a wet and muddy route, and anyone using it would miss seeing Place and St Anthony Church. So I advise you to take the official route up the lane past the gate to Place 2, to a stile about 250 yards (230 metres) from the slipway on the west side of the lane. Climb the stile, and head for St Anthony Church 3, noting how it is joined to Place House at the north transept. The south doorway is fine late-Norman work, and inside the tower arches are 13th century. Nikolaus Pevsner thought it 'the best example in the county of what a parish church was like in the 12th or 13th centuries'.

Walk up the slope and steps opposite the fine Norman south door, join a farm track, and descend to the creek-side past Place House. The present French-looking building was constructed in 1840 on the site of an Elizabethan house, which itself replaced a priory. The lawn in front was created in the middle of the last century from the mill pond of a tide mill, and the present sea wall was built where the tide mill dam once stood.

Herons may be seen along here, standing motionless in the water, waiting for a small fish or crab to come along. Before reaching Cellars Cottages, climb a stile and ascend a field to another stile at the top. Cellars Cottages served as pilchard cellars where the fish were processed before being exported to the Catholic countries of southern Europe.

From the stile a panoramic view opens to the north-west. St Mawes 1 with its castle occupies the middle distance, with Falmouth 2 miles (3.2 km) away across Carrick Roads. Descend to the foot of the field, and follow the Coast Path around Carricknath Point, then south towards St Anthony Head, with its lighthouse nearly at the water's edge **4**. This squat structure was built in 1834 as much to warn seafarers of the deadly Manacles reef to the south as to indicate the entrance to Falmouth Harbour. From 1882 to 1954 a bell, the largest in Cornwall, hung from the exterior below the lantern, and was rung in foggy conditions.

The Coast Path crosses a concrete dam dating from 1914, built to form a reservoir to provide water for St Anthony Battery **5**. The reservoir is now choked with silt. Below the dam are the small beaches of Great and Little Molunan, a lovely spot for a bathe at low tide.

Ignore the steep path climbing to the car park and stay low, entering a gate and contouring along a good path, past the old paraffin store, to the lighthouse. For safety's sake only enough fuel for its immediate needs was kept at the lighthouse, and the keepers carried it in churn-like containers suspended from wooden yokes. If time permits, and the lighthouse is open, a visit to climb the tower is strongly recommended.

From the lighthouse return for 50 yards (46 metres), climb the path to the car park and disused battery **5**, and turn south at the top. On the outside wall of the toilets, note the interpretive panel describing St Anthony Battery. The officers' quarters **6**

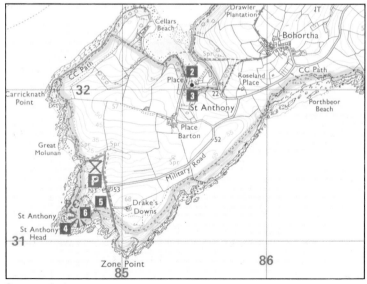

Contours are given in metres
The vertical interval is 5m

have been converted by the National Trust into comfortable holiday cottages, some of them suitable for disabled visitors. Old maps show a cliff castle or possibly a Roman signal station on the headland, but when the site was fortified in 1885 all traces of this earthwork disappeared.

On top of the gun apron the National Trust has erected a toposcope (viewfinder) which lines up places of interest and is accessible to people in wheelchairs. The Radford sisters, who are mentioned on the toposcope, were benefactors of the National Trust.

Leave this splendid viewpoint by heading south-east around Zone Point, the best place in the area for spotting sea birds. A prominent one-time coastguard signal station on Drake's Downs was demolished by the National Trust in 1985 as the wall ties had rusted through and rebuilding was uneconomical. The Coast Path follows the cliff edge with no fencing on the inland side, and this gives a feeling of freedom. It dips across a valley, and passes behind Porthbeor Beach, which is reached by a cliff path and linked to the nearby road by a permissive path.

Once past Porthbeor, the Coast Path wanders agreeably eastwards, turning north once round Killigerran Head, and reaches Towan Beach near a wreck post **7**, a relic of the days when the breeches buoy was employed by the coastguard service in ship rescues. It is a sturdy pole with climbing steps which simulated the mast of a ship in training exercises. A rocket was fired at the pole, the rope made fast, and the breeches buoy brought into play.

Towan is Cornish for sand dune, but as none exist there today it is safe to assume that a combination of the removal of sand to spread on the land to lighten the soil, and the consequent erosion of the beach-back by the sea, has caused the loss of stability in the low cliffs behind the beach. A short path links the beach with a car park and toilets at Porth. This was once a sanding road **8**. These are access tracks to beaches up which carts, packhorses and pannier-laden donkeys brought seaweed and sand to spread on the land as natural fertiliser. Over the years so much sand was removed that some Cornish beaches were seriously eroded.

North of Towan Beach the Coast Path keeps to the cliff edge and Portscatho **9** is reached without difficulty. Along this stretch you will see examples of the Cornish stile, a kind of stone cattle grid, and at the north end of Towan Beach there are three more sanding roads.

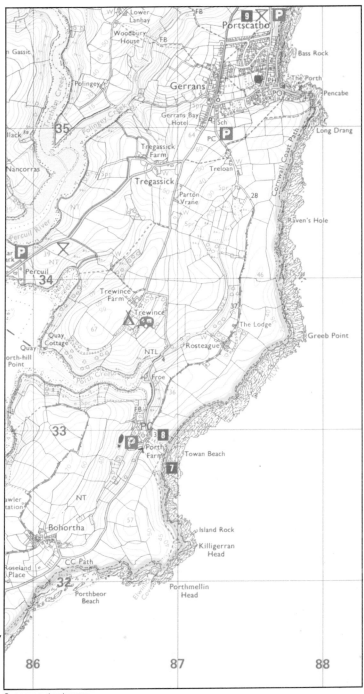

Contours are given in metres
The vertical interval is 5m

25

Froe Creek tide mill pond, near Towan Beach.

Portscatho **9** is an east-facing fishing village that now enjoys a Siamese-twin existence with Gerrans, the ancient parish centre up the hill. It boasts a good pub and some interesting little shops.

Leave the village along North Parade and pass through several fields down-slope from the main Portscatho car park. The Coast Path goes down a flight of stone steps into a steep, gullied track that descends to Porthcurnick Beach, and at low tide you can stroll across the strand to pick up the Coast Path at the far side. The taking of sand so reduced the level of Porthcurnick Beach that some cottages and a lime kiln were destroyed by the sea. At high tide you must pass behind the beach.

At the top of Porthcurnick Beach slipway, take the Coast Path going round Pednvadan, proceed north through several fields before passing into a wood containing many dead elms, then descend to Porthbean Beach. At high tide in a storm the beach gets washed by waves, but a track (still rough in summer 1988) bypasses the beach through wet scrub.

Leaving the beach after only about 10 yards (9 metres), turn up and take a right, sea-side, fork quite soon, to pass an isolated chalet. The Coast Path then passes through several more fields before descending to some small coves, and past a gate bearing a sign saying 'Curgurrel Farm Harbour'. Do not be misled by the grand name; this is only a slip leading to a tiny cove.

The Coast Path soon enters the National Trust property known as Treluggan Cliff, a scrubby slope through which the route wanders beguilingly. At the far end it turns briefly inland to circumvent the Pendower Hotel. At the road, turn right (south-east) and follow it past a car park to the road-end at the Pendower Beach House Hotel.

Here a lime kiln and a Second World War pillbox stand forlornly beside a very popular and safe beach which is a designated Eurobeach, complying fully with EEC standards. No sewage is discharged nearby.

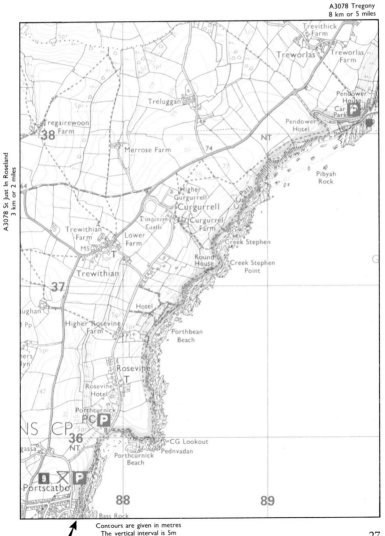

Contours are given in metres
The vertical interval is 5m

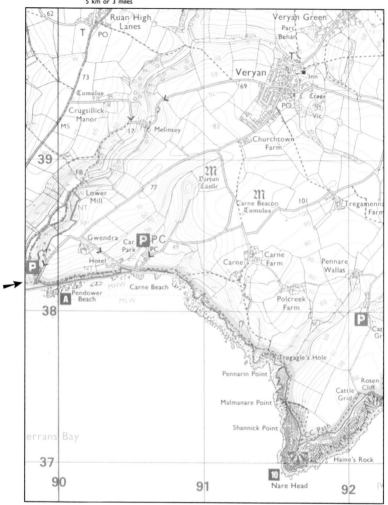

Contours are given in metres
The vertical interval is 5m

The route crosses the beach, or, at high tide, goes round the back of the beach to the car park, then climbs the road on the east side for a short distance before entering a field by a stile. This takes the walker along the low cliffs in front of the Nare Hotel to the road near Carne Beach, where there is another large car park and two Second World War pillboxes, both rather hard to spot. At low tide, Pendower Beach and Carne Beach coalesce, forming one long stretch of sand nearly a mile (1.5 km) long, and it is hard to say where Pendower ends and Carne begins. Follow the beach if you prefer **A**.

28

From the back of the large car park serving Carne Beach, a National Trust permissive footpath goes up the field to the prehistoric site known as Veryan Castle. It is positioned on the side of a hill and was presumably a settlement of some kind, although no dwelling remains have been found. About 400 yards (365 metres) to the east is Carne Beacon, one of the largest Bronze Age barrows in Britain. An excavation in 1855 revealed a stone cairn on top of a large cist (burial chamber) which contained ashes and charcoal. This site can be visited from a public footpath that passes the barrow.

From Carne Beach go up the road to the east, and round the hairpin bend turn right (east) over a stile signposted 'Portloe 3½'. The distance is all of that, and more! The Coast Path goes through a succession of fields. At the end of the second, look up left at the rocky crag near Carne Farm. (*Carn* is Cornish for a tor or natural pile of rocks.)

After a climb, the Coast Path descends steeply to Paradoe Cove (pronounced Prada) where a National Trust permissive path comes down the valley from the north-east. Here there are the remains of a fisherman's cottage on the south side of the cove. Once of two storeys and probably thatched, the walls above the ground floor are of cob, a mixture of clay and straw. The Coast Path climbs steeply out of the valley, and soon the crags of Nare Head beckon **10**.

This is a fine headland bristling with exposed igneous rock at its tip. In 1540 it was called Penare Point, with the accent on the second syllable, but over the years the unstressed first syllable was dropped.

The National Trust, as owner, was responsible for a great deal of tidying up and rationalisation of the farming landscape on Nare Head a few years ago. The agricultural buildings were old, scattered and unsuitable for modern farming, so the Trust, with help from the Ministry of Agriculture, built a completely new complex of buildings for the tenant, nearer to his house and in a natural hollow. The redundant structures were cleared away, a car park was built for visitors, a viewpoint provided, suitable for disabled people, and a new path opened from the car park down to Paradoe Cove. Several hundred trees were planted in this valley. Gull Rock, three-quarters of a mile (1.2 km) east of Nare Head, is a noted seabird nesting site.

The national trail skirts Nare Head, picks up a tractor track and goes north. Then the Coast Path bears round the cliff edge

Montbretia beside the Coast Path at Portloe.

and fence line. Follow the waymarks down **B**, and around Kiberick Cove. The curiously contoured field here is believed to have slipped 'once upon a time' and is called Slip Field. The Coast Path now rounds the Blouth and drops almost to sea level at Parc Caragloose Cove where a stream is crossed before climbing up a bracken slope, with a few zigzags thrown in for good measure.

The Coast Path now stays high around Manare Point before dropping down past a spiney ridge called The Jacka to the cosy village of Portloe **11**, which you reach close to the toilets. This must rate as one of the most unspoilt and attractive fishing villages in the whole of Britain. Very little new building has taken place to spoil it. As a harbour it is very cramped, and this was one reason why in the 17 years that there was a life-boat stationed at Portloe it did not perform a single service: in stormy weather the narrow entrance is too difficult for boats to negotiate.

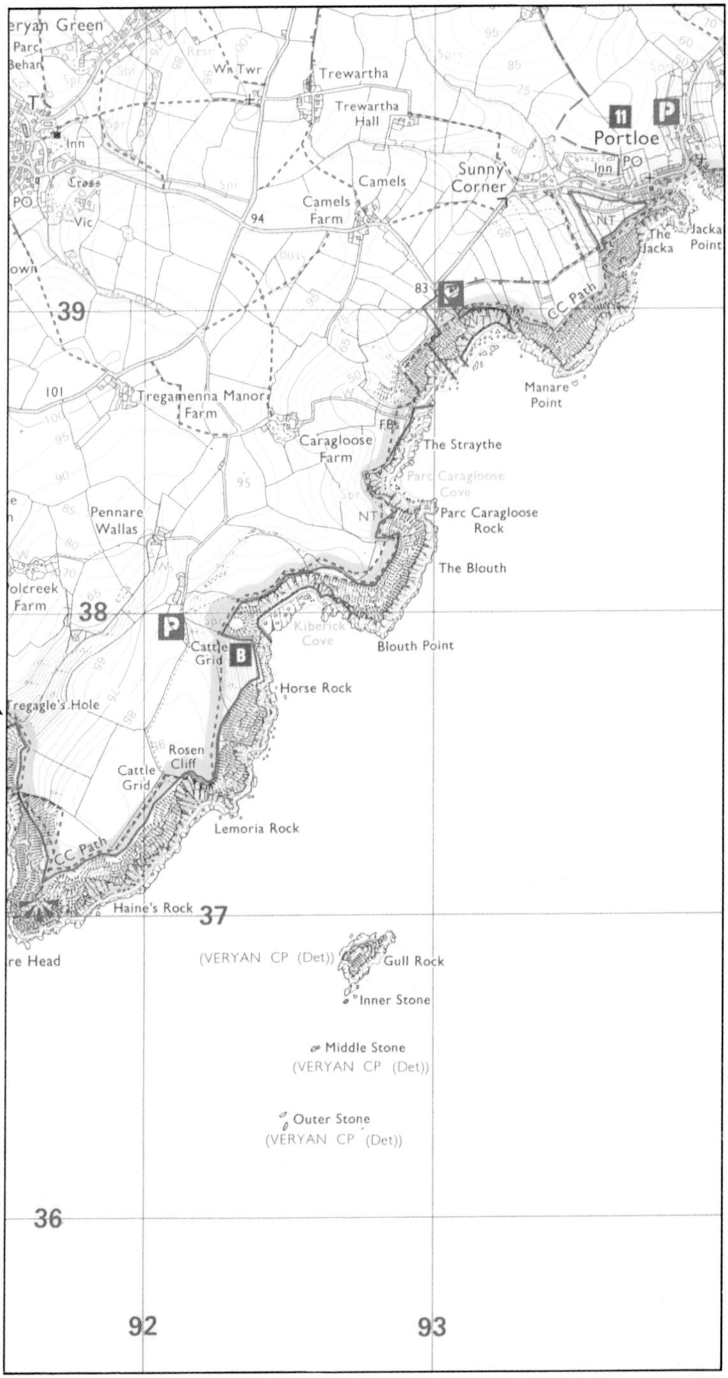

eryan Green
Parc Behan
Inn
Cross
PO
Vic
Wr Twr
Trewartha
Trewartha Hall
Camels
Camels Farm
94
Sunny Corner
Portloe
Inn
PO
NT
The Jacka
Jacka Point
VERYAN BAY
83
CC Path
NT
39
Manare Point
101
Tregamenna Manor Farm
FB
The Straythe
Caragloose Farm
Parc Caragloose Cove
Parc Caragloose Rock
NT
Pennare Wallas
The Blouth
Polcreek Farm
38
Kiberick Cove
Blouth Point
Cattle Grid
Horse Rock
Tregagle's Hole
Rosen Cliff
Cattle Grid
Lemoria Rock
CC Path
Haine's Rock
37
re Head
(VERYAN CP (Det))
Gull Rock
Inner Stone
Middle Stone
(VERYAN CP (Det))
Outer Stone
(VERYAN CP (Det))
36
92
93

Contours are given in metres
The vertical interval is 5m

A CIRCULAR WALK ROUND THE COAST AND CREEKS OF THE ROSELAND PENINSULA

5¾ miles (9.3 km)

From the National Trust car park at Porth, between Gerrans and St Anthony, walk down through the lower, grassy car parking area below and behind Towan Cottage. This leads to a footbridge over a stream, which gives access to a 2-mile (3.2-km) creekside path leading to Place slipway. At this point the beginning of the Coast Path is picked up (see page 22), and it may be followed past St Anthony Head and Zone Point, all the way round to Towan Beach, about another 4 miles (6.1 km). Turn inland here, and Porth car park is reached in 250 yards (230 metres).

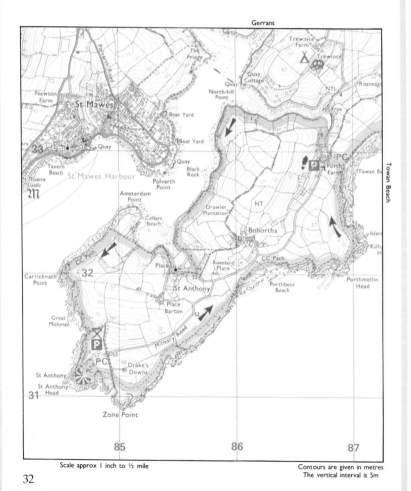

Scale approx 1 inch to ½ mile

Contours are given in metres
The vertical interval is 5m

Conserving the Cornish and South Devon Coasts

The Coast Path is formally designated by the Countryside Commission with the blessing of the government, but it is managed by Cornwall and Devon County Councils with substantial help from the Commission.

Much of the countryside through which the Path runs has been formally designated as an area of outstanding natural beauty by the Commission. This gives national recognition to the high quality of the landscape.

Heritage coasts

The need for measures to protect the undeveloped coast became a matter of some urgency just before the Second World War, when the ever-quickening pace of change was beginning to destroy the beauty of parts of Britain's rural coastline. During the war the government therefore appointed Professor Steers, the eminent coastal geographer, to assess the scenic quality of the unspoilt coastline of England and Wales.

It was more than 20 years before the government set in motion an official review. In 1970 the Countryside Commission reported back with a major proposal that 'the most scenically outstanding stretches of undeveloped coast be defined and protected as heritage coasts'.

By 1988 more than 30 per cent of the coastlines of England and Wales had been defined by the Commission in association with the local authorities, thus affording them special protection through planning, and a strong emphasis on practical action.

Much of the coast of Cornwall and Devon has been so defined, and there are three stretches between Plymouth and Falmouth. Heritage coast teams have been established to co-ordinate a wide range of conservation, recreation and interpretive tasks, and thus to assist in the management of the South West Coast Path. A leaflet about heritage coasts is obtainable from the Countryside Commission.

The National Trust

The National Trust (NT) is a charity, independent of government, founded in 1895 to acquire land and buildings for their permanent protection in England, Wales and Northern Ireland.

The Trust's first coastal acquisition in England was Barras Nose in North Cornwall in 1897, and the Dodman was given in 1919. Other properties followed in the 1920s and 1930s, but it

Looking east across the mouth of the Dart to the Mew Stone and Outer Froward

was not until after the Second World War that, with the increasing threats to the coastline, the need quickened to acquire further stretches.

Thus the NT launched Enterprise Neptune in 1965 with the aim of raising sufficient funds to acquire the 900 miles (1,448 km) of remaining unspoilt coastline in England, Wales and Northern Ireland. So far 500 miles (805 km) have been brought into NT ownership.

As you walk the Coast Path the boundary signs announce the NT's interest in many of the most beautiful stretches of land, not necessarily just rough cliff land, but sometimes extending a mile or so inland and including whole farms.

Point from Combe Point.

These major acquisitions meant that the NT was able to plan as a whole to the great advantage of the public, the tenant farmers and the landscape. Discreet new car parks and permissive link paths are provided, trees planted, and new farm buildings erected tucked into the hillsides.

So that the public can get the maximum enjoyment out of NT land, a series of interpretive leaflets is published by the two regions of the NT, Cornwall and Devon. These give maps of all the paths, and considerable detail about the history and wildlife of the area. A number of interpretive panels are also provided at selected locations. The NT now owns 110 miles (177 km) of the Cornish coast, and 76 miles (122 km) of the Devon coast.

2 Portloe to Charlestown

through Gorran Haven and Mevagissey
18¾ miles (30.1 km)

Portloe **11** grew as a settlement where two valleys converge at a narrow break in the cliffs. In the northern valley is a Methodist chapel. The present building dates from 1882. A previous building was struck by lightning in 1857 and badly damaged.

The Coast Path passes in front of the chapel **12** and some neighbouring cottages before climbing steeply to a small National Trust property known as The Old Flagstaff. Here an enclosure on the sea-side of the Coast Path represents all that is left of an early 19th century coastguard watch house.

The shattered craggy buttress of Hartriza Point is crossed. Like Nare Head and The Jacka it is composed of igneous rock, but this is the only obstacle to easy progress. A Shag Rock is passed offshore; there is another at St Anthony Head, but that

High tide at East Portholland. Note the double doors of the houses.

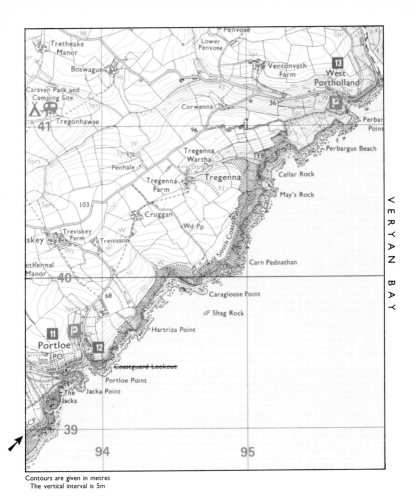

Contours are given in metres
The vertical interval is 5m

one is not shown on the map. You may like to note how repetitious some place names are as you progress eastwards. Usually several miles separate the same place name. Curiously, a Caragloose Point three-quarters of a mile (1.2 km) north-east of Portloe repeats a name found 1 mile (1.6 km) south-west of that village. As you near West Portholland you will see some once-cultivated fields. In times past, Cornwall's marginal cliff slopes were often planted with crops.

The Coast Path descends to the twin villages of West and East Portholland **13**, each standing behind a beach and in its own valley. They are joined by a road along which the Coast Path is routed. West Portholland is the smaller of the two villages and consists of a Methodist chapel, a lime kiln, fishing sheds and a

Caerhays Castle at Porthluney Cove.

few dwellings. East Portholland is a little larger, and has a post office and shop, and used to have a pub called The Cutter. There was a Methodist chapel here, too, but it closed in 1938. Mills once employed the water power flowing down the valleys. Note how the easternmost cottages in East Portholland are shuttered against breaking waves.

The Coast Path climbs up near these cottages and follows an uncomplicated route to a gate leading into a field. Go through the gate, turn right, and follow the field edge down, along, and up to a stile giving access to the road by a hairpin bend just west of Porthluney Cove.

As you walk down from the gate, the ruined building above you and to your left is a one-time coastguard watch house. It is on private land and should not be approached. After you meet the road and are walking down to the cove, a ruin visible from a gate and almost hidden in ivy and undergrowth is probably a folly. This also is on private land and may be viewed only from the road.

Porthluney Cove is a clean and healthy stretch of sand, offering safe bathing, and is a designated Eurobeach. Behind the beach are the grounds of Caerhays Castle **14**. Designed in

1808 by John Nash, who was responsible for Buckingham Palace and the Brighton Pavilion, this picturesque mansion stands in splendid grounds, which are sometimes open for charity and famous for their flowering shrubs.

Walk east behind the beach and climb a stile into parkland just after a lodge. The Coast Path bears south, and there is a lengthy climb before the first rise is surmounted. From this the next headland, Greeb Point, looks like a crocodile's snout.

National Trust land is entered at Lambsowden Cove, but Greeb Point is not Trust-owned. Once over the spine of Greeb

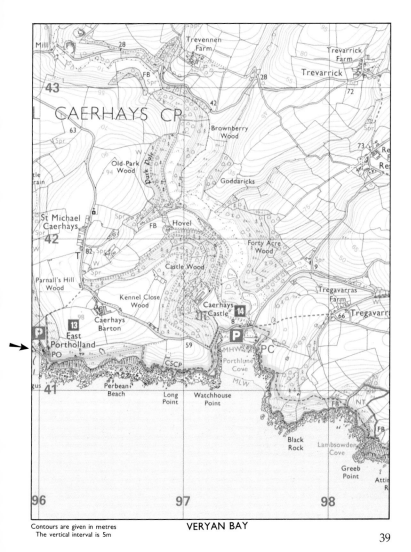

Contours are given in metres
The vertical interval is 5m

VERYAN BAY

Point the path is clear and pleasant as it rambles down (mostly) to Hemmick Beach. Boswinger Youth Hostel is half a mile (800 metres) up the road to the north.

Hemmick Beach is one of Cornwall's most beautiful coves. South-west-facing, with rock pools, sand and no commercialisation, it should be reached – if not by the Coast Path – by walking down from the National Trust car park in the hamlet of Penare. There is no room for cars behind the beach, and the approach lanes are narrow and exceedingly steep.

A few yards up the road to the south of Hemmick Beach, a stile gives access to the Coast Path once more. There is initially a steep climb, then the path levels out, dips again, and climbs to the famous long earthwork on Dodman Point called the Balk, Baulk or Bulwark **15**. This is an Iron Age earthwork on a grand scale. Two somewhat flattened Bronze Age barrows lie within the area. No dwelling sites have been found so far, but the remains of a medieval field system can be seen.

Having reached the top of the headland, the Coast Path now pleasantly contours the upper slopes to the tip of this noble promontory with its massive stone cross and well-preserved watch house **16**. Dodman Point, or the Dodman as it is usually called, is the most striking headland on the South Cornish coast.

Hemmick Beach seen from the Coast Path, with Boswinger visible on the skyline.

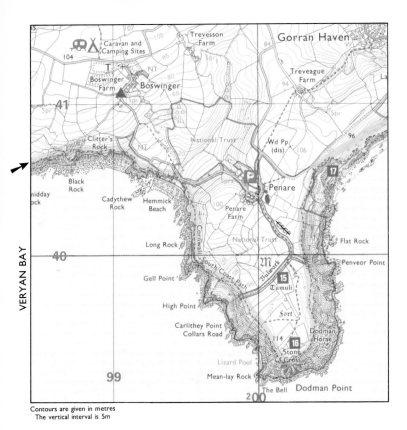

Contours are given in metres
The vertical interval is 5m

Over the years it has caused numerous wrecks. The granite cross was built in 1896 by a local parson as a seamark, but unhappily it failed to save the destroyers *Thrasher* and *Lynx* from hitting rocks on the south-west side in fog a year later. A more recent tragedy was the pleasure boat *Darlwin*, which sank with all its passengers in 1966. A few yards inland from the Coast Path, and rather lost among the scrub, is a carefully preserved late 18th century coastguard watch house, with its pulpit look-out alongside, and the only one of its kind on the Cornish coast.

The lower path option should now be taken. From near the cross it soon heads north along the east side of the Dodman, entering a large enclosure by a stile, and then passing the east end of the earthwork mentioned above. The path carries on north, almost meets the road, at a place called The Gruda **17**, then slants along eastwards above the elegant parabola of Vault Beach. Hang-gliding is sometimes indulged in from The Gruda, which is a length of unfenced road.

Gorran Haven is near at hand, and a pleasant stroll round the rocky projection of Maenease Point soon brings the walker to this rapidly growing village. There is a high and low path round the point, but the higher one has little extra to commend it, except an opportunity to see a plaque that remembers Sir John Fischer Williams of Lamledra, 'jurist and man of letters' who died in 1947. The plaque is fixed to an east-facing rock at the northern end of the higher path.

The Coast Path reaches Gorran Haven **18** down Foxhole Lane. As you descend, note the terrace of old coastguard cottages on the opposite hillside, although the more recent extensive bungaloid growth may catch the eye to the exclusion of such features as Victorian buildings. Gorran Haven is reached by the Gorran Playgroup building. Originally Porth Just, and later corrupted into Porth East, the place is the the 'haven' of Gorran, the parish centre situated 1 mile (1.6 km) inland. Fishing, and crabbing in particular, was the local calling, but, as a glance at the hillsides around the village will show, Gorran Haven is now a residential area for retired people and for those who work in St Austell.

To leave Gorran Haven, walk north up Church Street and turn into Cliff Road. Do not follow the signposted footpath near the bottom of Church Street. A stile is climbed at the end of Cliff Road by the entrance to the last house, and for much of the way to Chapel Point the Coast Path is separated from the fields by a fence. This simplifies route-finding but gives the walker a hemmed-in feeling. Along this stretch of path you may hear a bell-buoy tolling out to sea. At Great Perhaver, tunnels driven into the cliff were used to mine ochre, a material used in paint. An iron gantry was built as a loading quay for the ships that carried the mineral away at high tide.

Carn Rocks is a distinctive feature but the site shown on the map as 'earthwork' barely shows above ground level. Around the next headland, Turbot Point, is a small piece of cliff land, owned by the National Trust, and called Bodrugan's Leap **19**. Tradition states that here Sir Henry Trenowth of nearby Bodrugan, pursued by his enemy Sir Richard Edgcumbe of Cotehele, leapt into the sea and a waiting boat to escape to France during the reign of Henry VII.

Chapel Point now catches the eye, not for its natural appearance, but because of the three striking houses which were designed by John A. Campbell and built between 1933 and 1938 of stone taken from the site.

The Coast Path cuts across the neck of Chapel Point and carries on to rejoin the cliff top, before briefly entering a small scrubby wood, then follows the Chapel Point track, which leads to the road south of Portmellon. Now a part of Mevagissey, this was formerly a boat-building and fishing centre. In 1849 many Mevagissey people fled to Portmellon during a cholera epidemic, and were accommodated in tents on the north side of the bay. From time to time the road is inundated by the sea, and in 1969 it was totally washed away.

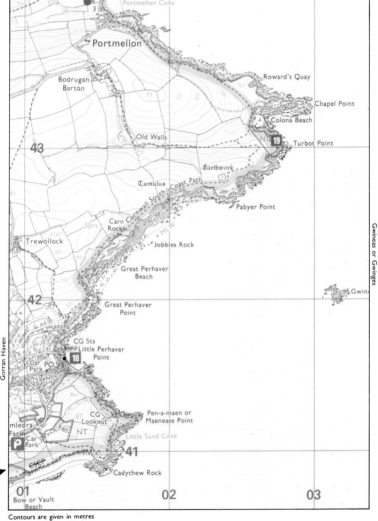

Contours are given in metres
The vertical interval is 5m

Now take the road to Mevagissey; the two places are really one built-up area. As you walk into Mevagissey you can get off the road by passing through a small park overlooking the harbour. This sheltered fishing town repays a leisurely stroll around its back streets and waterfront, and a visit to the museum is strongly recommended. The first pier was built in 1430, but Mevagissey began to assume its present appearance in the late 18th century when the inner harbour was built. The outer harbour is only about a hundred years old.

As you leave Mevagissey heading north you pass the site of a Napoleonic War gun battery, although the guns are now used as mooring bollards on the quays below, and just above was one of Mevagissey's two ropewalks, where ropes were made for the local ships.

To leave the town, climb steeply up behind the toilets on the north side of the inner harbour, past the coastguard station. The Coast Path crosses a public open space, and you make for the eastern end of a terrace facing you. Take care to avoid what the local dogs have left behind. Another hazard is the declared risk of cliff falls.

After a series of ups and downs you will see ahead of you the massed ranks of caravans at Pentewan, and across the bay is the reptilian hump of Black Head. Deserted Portgiskey is an interesting place, a tantalising jumble of pilchard cellars, terraces, gardens and small fields. Up the valley the skeletal trees remind one of what we lost during the outbreak of Dutch elm disease.

Once past Portgiskey the Coast Path follows a bank beside and above the B3273, and hugs it closely to join the road at the entrance to Pentewan Sands Caravan and Camping Site. Follow the road, leaving it where it is signposted Pentewan and going along West End. Pentewan **20** is an interesting place as it is an artificial harbour (see page 49).

From the square, walk up Pentewan Hill for 100 yards (90 metres), and turn right along the Terrace. This is a pleasant, unspoilt row of houses with a church at the far end. Beyond the church, a signpost indicates the way to go. The Coast Path climbs between fences, and passes a concrete Second World War gun emplacement on the seaward side, from where there is a good view of the now blocked harbour outlet to the sea.

This stretch of the Coast Path is strenuous, with many hills. The cliffs of Polrudden Cove provide favourite nesting sites for fulmars, and just beyond is a quarry entrance (disused) for the famous Pentewan stone. There were other quarries to the west.

Hay Wood
Polglaze
Porthtowan
Spr

Caravan and Camping Site
Hay

48
MS

Glentowan

Adit Quarries (dis)

Quarry (dis)
Cornwall South Coast Pa

Quarry (dis)

New Road Plantation
Polrudden Farm

Polrudden Cove

PO
Pentewan
Point of Well

Barton Farm
4
20

PH
Gamas Point

47
Spr

Caravan Park and Camping Site
Pentewan Beach

T
Winnick

Sconhoe Beach

Mean High Water
Mean Low Water

Resr
Tregiskey

Tregiskey Farm
79

Portgiskey

46

Cornwall South Coast Path

Trewinney

Cheesewarne Farm

Penare Point

Cemy

FB

Quarry (dis)

Treleaven Farm
Cemy
Sch

Polstreath

AGISSEY CP
F Sta

45

MEVAGISSEY

CG Sta
Perunys
PO
Mus

82

Stuckumb Point

Wd Pp (dis)

Polkirt Beach

01
Penwarne
02

T

Contours are given in metres
The vertical interval is 5m

MEVAGISSEY BAY

At The Vans, a wooded area, the Coast Path descends to a stream, meets another path coming from inland, and reaches Hallane Mill Beach. (There is in fact no need to go right down to the beach, but it makes a pleasant diversion.)

Black Head is the next goal, a distinctive promontory that has been in view for many miles past. This was bought by the National Trust in 1986. As might be expected, it was turned into a cliff castle in Iron Age times by the simple means of banking and ditching the isthmus. A path goes out to the top of Black Head, but the walker pressed for time can bypass this bonus by turning north and following the fenced-off path towards Trenarren. At the foot of the wooded cliff slope is another one-time pilchard station, Ropehaven **21**, not accessible by a public right of way.

Outside Trenarren House there is a small parking area, and at the north end a stile gives access to one of the most tiring lengths of Coast Path in this section – a real switchback. Despite being so close to St Austell, this is a quiet and very rural part of the coast. Features to note are the place name Silvermine Point, and a rock arch to the north of Phoebe's Point. And then, suddenly, you are free-wheeling down to Porth Pean or Porthpean. The name means 'little harbour', in contrast to the 'great harbour' of Polmear, the Cornish name for Charlestown, three-quarters of a mile (1.2 km) to the north-east.

The Coast Path climbs steep steps at the north end of the beach and passes a two-storey Second World War lookout. A public open space is crossed, and then a route is followed above Du Porth Cliffs and behind the gardens of houses. You are now nearly at Charlestown. Pass behind a headland and descend to the harbour by the seaward terrace of this fascinating place.

What we now call Charlestown **22** began life as West Polmear (or Porthmeor), but it was then simply a small cove. In 1790 the population numbered nine, by 1801 it was 281 and 50 years later nearly 3,000 people lived in the newly built village. The place was now Charlestown, after Charles Rashleigh, the local mining entrepreneur who had invested his capital in creating this harbour to serve the St Austell china clay industry and the copper mines. Around the lock-gated harbour, which was excavated out of the solid rock, Rashleigh established other industries: lime-burning, shipbuilding, brickmaking, net and bark houses, a rope walk and pilchard cellars.

Anyone with time to spare will find a visit to Charlestown visitor centre and Shipwreck Museum a fascinating experience.

Sch
ona Stone

Cemetery Shaft
(dis)

52

Shaft
(dis)

Mine
(disused)

77

74

Shaft
(dis)

Duporth

22

Charlestown

PO PH

CSCP

Lock

Docks

Appletree
Point

Coastguard
Lookout

Landrion
Point

Shaft
(dis)

Gull

Polmear Island

Holiday
Resort

Du Porth

51 86

Quarry
(dis)

41

Carrickowel Point

Lower
Porthpean

Porth Pean

P

PO

Robin's Rock

Higher
Porthpean

Flat Rock

50

Sprs

Phoebe's Point

Castle Gotha
Farm

Silvermine Point

Castle Gotha
Settlement

Sprs

Gwendra Point

CSCP

104

49

P

Ropehaven

21

Ledrah

Gerrans Point

Trenarren

84

ick

H Ram

75

70

Hallane

65

The Bite

03

The Vans

04

05

htowan Spr

Drennick

Fort

Black Head

48

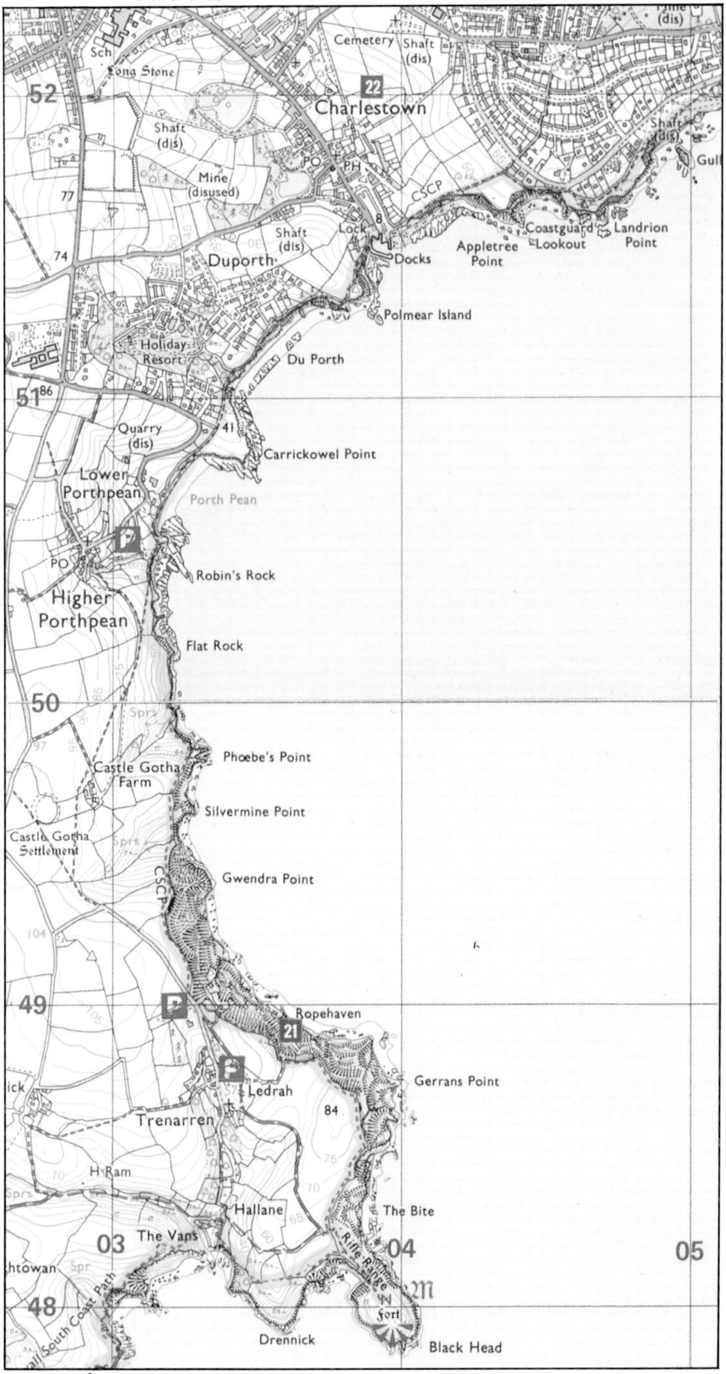

ST AUSTELL BAY

Cornwall South Coast Path

Contours are given in metres
The vertical interval is 5m

47

A circular walk round Dodman Point

2 miles (3.2 km), with a possible extension of 2¼ miles (3.6 km)

From the National Trust car park in the tucked-away hamlet of Penare, at the base of Dodman Point, or the Dodman, walk south along the farm track, turning right at the earthwork. When you reach the Coast Path, follow it round to the point and continue round, now heading north, past the eastern end of the earthwork, to The Gruda **17**, the unfenced road overlooking Vault Beach. Get up on to the road, turn left, go round the corner and, by a gate, climb the stile left, and cross the field to Penare and the car park.

This walk can be extended by 2¼ miles (3.6 km) by carrying on east instead of joining the road at The Gruda. Then go round Maenease Point to Gorran Haven (see page 42), before returning along the road to The Gruda **17**, round the corner, then over the stile and across the field back to the car park.

Contours are given in metres
The vertical interval is 5m

Pentewan

Pentewan **20** is the first of South Cornwall's three planned harbours you see as you walk from west to east; the others are Charlestown and Par. While the village is pleasant and well cared for, the harbour appears neglected by comparison. Its demise is largely the result of the sea choking the channel with sand.

The earliest harbour was built here in 1744 by the Hawkins family, but the present basin, quays and outlet to the sea were begun in 1820. Throughout its life the harbour was troubled by sand build-up and by china clay silt coming down the St Austell River, so the trade responsible for the port was largely responsible for its closure. The last china clay cargo left Pentewan in 1929, but shipments of sand continued outwards, with timber, coal, fertiliser and cement coming in. The railway was taken up in the First World War, so all the later cargoes were removed from Pentewan by road.

Pentewan was, of course, the source of Pentewan stone, a hard, fine-grained stone much used in the local buildings and wharves, and employed in local churches as an interior and exterior material. One quarry, marked 'disused' on the map, will be seen beside the Coast Path on the way to Black Head.

Pilchard fishing

Seasonal pilchard fishing was carried on by the Cornish for hundreds of years until the shoals began to disappear in the last century. The fish were processed in fish cellars, and almost every inlet, and certainly every port, had its fishery. In the cellars the fish were packed in layers with salt and pressed to extract the oil. The square-cut holes in the side of cellar buildings were to receive one end of the timber press. The other end was weighted with a rock. After three or four weeks of pressing, the fish were packed into barrels for export. This trade gave employment to many, but the pervasive smell kept visitors at bay.

3 Charlestown to Fowey

through Polkerris and around the Gribbin
9¾ miles (15.6 km)

The first half of this section is probably the least appealing stretch of the walk between Falmouth and Exmouth, but better things follow.

The Coast Path may be picked up east of Charlestown **22** by crossing the catwalk on top of the lock gate, providing the gate is closed! The outer harbour is very attractive, with aesthetically satisfying granite bollards and steps.

Walk up the cliff path towards the toilets, noticing the line of square holes between granite blocks in the outer wall of the building on your left (north), used for pilchard pressing.

Pass through a kissing gate into a field and follow the field edge to another kissing gate by a seat. Ignore the field edge here, and carry straight on to a third kissing gate where you should turn right (south). Follow the top field edge to the fourth kissing gate and carry on along the path to the point where it emerges on a road opposite the Porth Avallen Hotel. Follow the road for 80 yards (75 metres), and turn right (south-east).

The Coast Path follows the cliff edge and is confined. Where it meets a manicured open space, the path goes to the far end and passes in front of the large Carlyon Bay Hotel. Here you keep a fence to your left (north) and an open space to your right (south). Descend to a car park and pass down its seaward side.

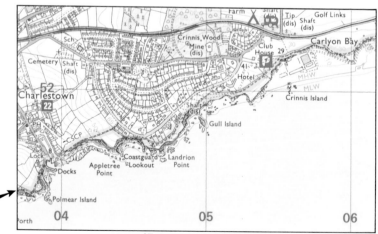

ST AUSTELL BAY

Contours are given in metres
The vertical interval is 5m

The route now runs along the top of the cliffs, with the Carlyon Bay Hotel Golf Club on the left (north), and the main railway line between London and Penzance just beyond. As you proceed east, look down into the next indentation in the cliffs and you will see the track of a miniature railway.

The path gradually drops to Spit Point at the far end of the golf course. Ahead are the chimneys and paraphernalia of the china clay works, and the view beyond is of the pleasant unspoilt coastline between Polmear and the Gribbin, with the tiny village of Polkerris punctuating the cliffs. At Spit Point the path turns inland along a narrow double-fenced tarmac path which passes through the works.

Turn left (north) under the railway, and emerge on to the A3082 beside an old chimney. There you will see a Coast Path signpost. Turn right (north-east) along this busy road – there is no alternative – and after going beneath the railway twice, turn right (east) again over a level crossing, and carry on along a flat, straight residential road lined with a scattering of shops. This is Par.

Just east of the Welcome Home Inn the route goes off right (south) to the beach and on to Polmear. However, an alternative route that stays on the road is more straightforward, and leads directly to Polmear where, just to the east of the Ship Inn, and between it and the well-restored Rashleigh Cottages **23**, the Coast Path sets off uphill.

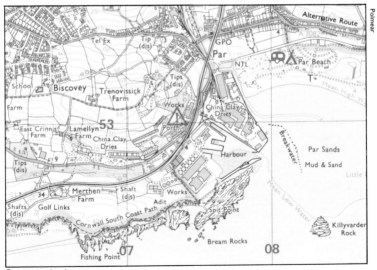

Contours are given in metres
The vertical interval is 5m

After about 200 yards (180 metres), climb the wall right (west). A signpost here bears the Saints' Way waymark **24**. This modern reconstruction of a possible Dark Age (AD 400–700) route between Fowey and Padstow imaginatively suggests that Celtic clerics and merchants travelled this way in preference to the sea journey around Land's End. A locally produced guide-book describes the route. Now follow the clearly defined Coast Path to Polkerris. On the first bit of this stretch there are two ways down from the path, to the car park and to the beach at low-tide mark.

The Coast Path descends to the car park of the Rashleigh Inn at Polkerris **25**, which is one of Cornwall's most perfect fishing villages. Tucked into the bottom of a narrow valley, Polkerris has been saved from modern development by benign owner-ship. A pub, a café (in season) which occupies the old lifeboat house, and a straggle of cottages behind make up the village. But the castle-like pilchard cellars above the harbour, now neglected, were the *raison d'être* for Polkerris.

The Coast Path now ascends southwards from the slip on the south side of the village. It zigzags steeply through garlic-smelling sycamore woods and, reaching the top above the harbour, gives a good view of the setting of Polkerris.

There now follows 1½ miles (2.4 km) of easily traced Coast Path all the way to the Gribbin **26**, or Gribbin Head as it appears on maps. A loop path descends in front of the Daymark, but the true route is to proceed north-east and take the path leading to Polridmouth **27**, which is visible half a mile (800 metres) away.

The 84-foot (26-metre) red and white candy-striped Daymark was built in 1832 by Trinity House (the lighthouse and lightship authority) to enable sailors to distinguish the Gribbin from other South Cornish headlands. Unusually for Cornwall, the Gribbin bears much woodland, a mixture of sycamore, holly, beech and *Rhododendron ponticum*. The sea buckthorn, a prickly shrub with orange berries in the autumn, grows on the western side.

Polridmouth **27**, or Pridmth, has two sandy coves separated by a low bluff. The second (easterly) one has a lake behind it, and you must cross to the wooded slope beyond by the dam. Those who are not walking the Coast Path can easily reach Polridmouth down a farm track from a car park at Menabilly Barton. The beach house behind the easterly cove is the original dwelling that gave Daphne du Maurier the inspiration for *Rebecca*. 'Manderley' is really Menabilly, up the valley, where the author lived for many years.

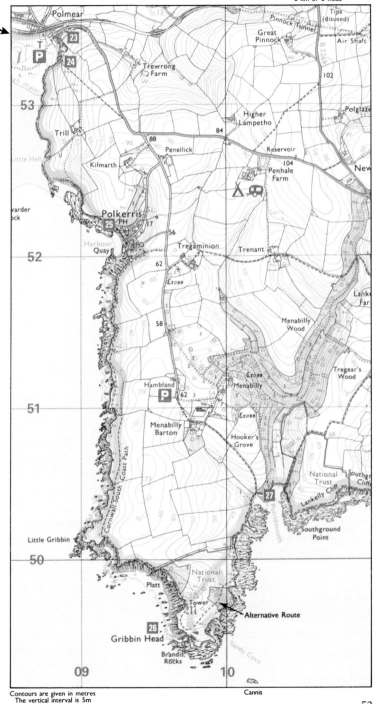

Polmear

23

T
P

24

Trewrong
Farm

53

Trill

Little Hell

Kilmarth

Penellick

88

Higher
Lampetho

84

Reservoir

104
Penhale
Farm

102

Polglaze

New

warder
ock

Polkerris
PH

25

Harbour
Quay

52

17

56

62

Cross

58

Hambland

P

62

Menabilly
Barton

51

Tregaminion

Cross
Menabilly

Cross

Hooker's
Grove

Trenant

Menabilly
Wood

Tregear's
Wood

Lanke
Far

73

70

65

Cornwall South Coast Path

Little Gribbin

50

National
Trust

Lankelly Cliff

27

Polridmouth

Southground
Point

Southgr
Cliff

National
Trust

Platt

National
Trust

Tower
21

Alternative Route

26
Gribbin Head

Brandis
Rocks

Sandy Cove

Cannis

09

10

Contours are given in metres
The vertical interval is 5m

53

The Coast Path continues up and down, and there are two more small coves before Fowey is reached, where access to the beach is possible. The second is Coombe Haven (or Hawne). The path passes through Allday's Fields, given to Fowey in 1951, then enters woods to drop down to Readymoney Cove. You may wish to turn right (east) and follow a small path down and around to see St Catherine's Castle **28**, then return to the Coast Path.

The castle was built in 1540 by Thomas Treffry as one of the defences planned by Henry VIII along the south coast. It is now owned by English Heritage. The strange stone coronet inside protective railings above the castle is the Rashleigh Mausoleum, resting place of William Rashleigh, his wife and daughter.

The main path descends through Covington Woods, then turns right (east) at the bottom where Love Lane begins. There is another Saints' Way waymark here. From Readymoney Cove it is a simple walk into Fowey (pronounced 'Foy') and the foot ferry to Polruan.

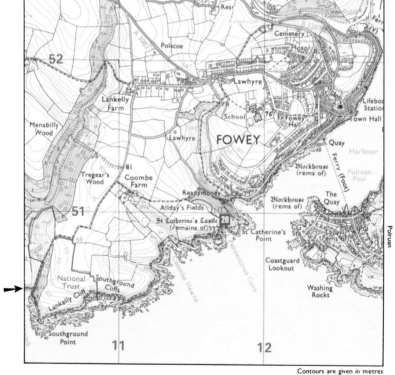

Contours are given in metres
The vertical interval is 5m

Par china clay works and harbour

Devon and Cornwall have the total UK reserves of this useful white mineral – china clay – whose extraction so strikes the northern visitor used to coal tips and slag heaps.

Apart from its use in the ceramic industry – china, porcelain, tiles, and sanitary ware – china clay is also used in the manufacture of paper, and the pages of this book contain a proportion of it, as a filler and whitener. Cosmetics, paint, rubber, crayons and many other commodities requiring a chemically inert filler use this rare mineral.

Par harbour was begun by J.T. Treffry – yet another of the Cornish industrialists who changed the face of early 19th century Cornwall – but 20th century expansion has totally changed its appearance. It is, of course, a shallow harbour and while it can accommodate more ships than Fowey, the latter benefits from a deep-water harbour at all states of the tide.

Fowey

Fowey enjoys the kind of situation at the mouth of a deep-water inlet that you will see again further east at Salcombe and Dartmouth.

The centre of the town is just below the fine church, which boasts a clerestory, a rare feature in Cornish churches. Here the life of the town pulsates, and there are pubs, restaurants and hotels. Near the church is Place, the family home of the Treffry family for over 500 years.

History tells us that Fowey was the focus of a rough and tumble in 1457 when the French landed and set fire to the port. Fowey men had long been aggressive marauding sailors, adopting a corsair-like approach to their private wars with France, so it was hardly surprising that the French decided on revenge. It failed to have any effect.

In 1469 John Willcock, a local captain, captured fifteen ships off the Brittany coast in a fortnight. This lawlessness embarrassed Edward IV as he had just made peace with the French, so he sent a messenger to Fowey to tell the inhabitants to desist. The hapless emissary was sent back minus an ear.

Fowey is still a port, and large ships laden with china clay depart from wharves north of the town to destinations all over the world. There is a youth hostel at Penquite, Golant, about 3½ miles (5.6 km) north of Fowey.

Looking down Polruan's narrow main street to Fowey.

4 Polruan to Looe

passing through Polperro
11¾ miles (18.8 km)

This is one of the finest stretches of walking between Falmouth and Exmouth.

Having crossed by the foot ferry from Fowey it is worth having a look at Polruan before setting off. Polruan is to Fowey what Kingswear is to Dartmouth. In the late 20th century both are smaller versions of their twins across the water, but it is likely that Polruan has a more ancient history than Fowey.

From the quay walk up the short hill to the foot of the steep main street, then turn sharp right along West Street. Now turn up Battery Lane, past the coastguard station, and on to an open space where there is a coastguard lookout. From here there are fine views westwards of the coast to the Gribbin and the Dodman.

Where a fork occurs in the path, take the higher (inland) one, as the lower path goes down only to the Washing Rocks. The Coast Path passes a large, old vertical wall on the highest point by a less ancient watch house. This is all that remains of St Saviour's Chapel, probably built as a seamark.

Walk east through the village car park approach, then bear right down a signposted lane to the coastal fields. The path is now clear and Polruan is left behind.

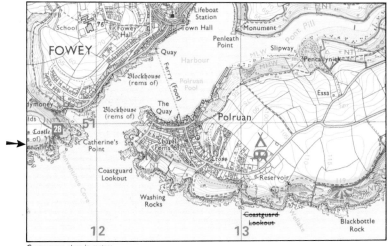

Contours are given in metres
The vertical interval is 5m

The Coast Path climbs, and enters National Trust land at Blackbottle Rock (surely a smuggling reference!). Where the Coast Path enters Trust land note the doggie stile devised by National Trust warden Leslie Hicks. A simple lifting device enables owners to pass their possibly elderly and probably muddy dogs through the barrier without having to lift them. At the highest point a seat is reached, a good place to take in the view of Pencarrow Head. Thrift grows here in season, and foxgloves line the path like a wedding guard of honour.

The path dips to pass round Lantic Bay, and a short link path heads inland by a National Trust moneybox to join the east-to-west hinterland road. It passes a now disused tip on which exotic plants are known to bloom. The Coast Path climbs steeply above Great Lantic Beach to meet another link path coming from the road and a strategically sited car park, then turns 90 degrees to the south with a high and a low option towards Pencarrow Head. A steep path cuts down the cliffside to the beach, which is free of sewage but may have an undertow.

To the east of Pencarrow Head, a satisfying promontory with some jutting rocky outcrops, the path passes behind a privately occupied 19th century watch house, best seen from the other side of Lantivet Bay, before turning due east. At this point another path goes inland to a large car park at Frogmore, which has the extra facility of toilets.

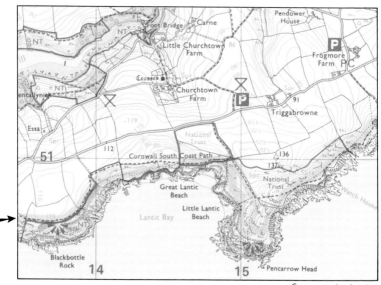

Contours are given in metres
The vertical interval is 5m

A scramble path descends to a low-tide cove west of Sandheap Point – Palace Cove – where there are the scant remains of a pilchard palace or cellar. The Coast Path then drops steeply to Lansallos Cove **29**, an unspoilt inlet that can also be reached by a delightful lane from Lansallos village. No sewage is discharged near this beach.

Local farmers of perhaps 200 years ago were responsible for the curious cutting at the back of this beautiful little bay. It enabled them to get their small carts and pack animals down to the beach to collect sand and seaweed for the land. A water mill stood nearby and disappeared only in the last 25 years or so.

To proceed east there are two options. At low tide, a path ascends from the foot of the beach, climbing steeply up the promontory to overlook Parson's Cove, then bearing east to reach the Coast Path. The alternative is to walk up the valley for 200 yards (180 metres) to a wicket gate, then turn right (south) along a track, entering a field briefly, and meeting the other path by a stile built between stone posts.

The Coast Path now heads east with no route-finding problems for 2 miles (3.2 km), although there are severe gradients. The Lansallos National Trust land is left behind at East Coombe at a wooden footbridge, and from here a three-quarter-mile (1.2-km) National Trust permissive path goes up the valley to the road at Windsor Farm.

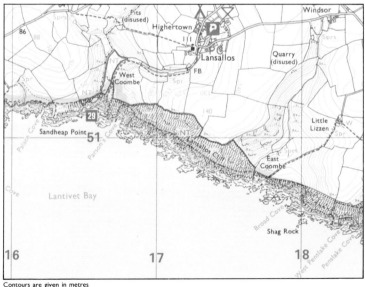

Contours are given in metres
The vertical interval is 5m

Beyond the stream a public right of way leaves the Coast Path and slants steeply north-east to the derelict building of Little Lizzen, used at one time by Marie Stopes, the pioneer of birth control, as a holiday cottage. The white Daymark beside the path lines up with a white mark lower down the cliff to warn boats of the Udder Rock out to sea. The Udder Rock bell-buoy may be heard tolling its solemn warning. The rock itself is exposed at very low tides.

From the Raphael Cliff National Trust sign a natural rock arch is visible at sea level. The next sign announces Chapel Cliff, pronounced 'Chaypel', where a path heading upwards gets one to Polperro by the expenditure of more energy than if one remains on the lower path, and to little advantage. There are, in fact, three parallel routes at one point with linking paths, so anyone spending a few days in the area should bear these extra routes in mind.

The true (lower) Coast Path passes a bad-weather shelter – or is it a summer house? Where the higher path rejoins the lower, some overgrown cultivation plots and fish-drying huts will be noticed, and two more shelters will be seen further on.

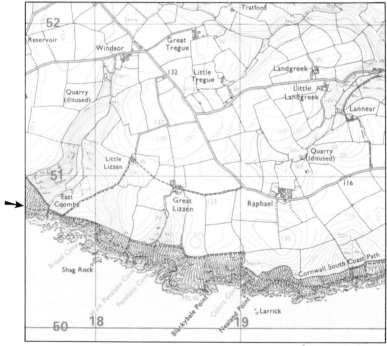

Contours are given in metres
The vertical interval is 5m

As you near the mouth of Polperro harbour, the large shed standing in the lee of Peak Rock is the net loft, now owned by the National Trust but once the building where fishermen stored and maintained their nets. The path drops down to the harbour either on the seaward side of the Three Pilchards Inn or near the Blue Peter Café: it splits in two, but the destination is the same. Polperro is best seen when the tide is in and the waterfront houses seem to float on the water.

To leave Polperro, walk round the north side of the harbour, past a pleasant sitting-out area, and take the higher path at a fork. The lower path is Reuben's Walk, named after a local man, Reuben Oliver, who was Polperro's harbourmaster. A steep path comes down from Brent, an estate to the north, and there are private cultivation plots beside the path. At the next fork stay low, and the shared War Memorial for Talland and Polperro is reached at Downend Point. Two pairs of black and white striped beacons (shown on the map as 'landmarks') to the east delineate a nautical measured mile for speed trials offshore.

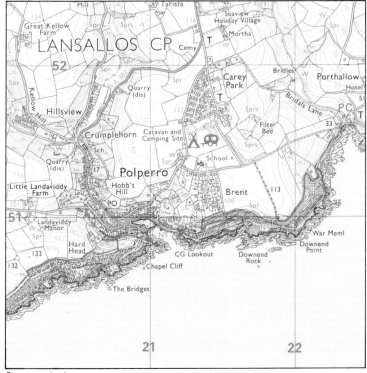

Contours are given in metres
The vertical interval is 5m

The inner harbour at Polperro.

The path, much used by local walkers, carries on round Talland Bay, joins a house drive, follows a green corridor, then drops steeply down to the beach, Talland Bay West, which gives safe bathing free from sewage. Over the low headland, Talland Bay East is smaller. A short distance up the lane from here and worth visiting is Talland Church, which is chiefly remarkable for its detached tower and old bench-ends. Talland House was the inspirational home of the novelist Francis Brett-Young.

The Coast Path now strikes out to an unnamed promontory which the National Trust has designated Hendersick on its omega signs, after the nearby farm of that name. Along this stretch you may be aware for the first time of the Eddystone Lighthouse 14 miles (22.5 km) to the south-east.

Once at the tip of the point, St George's Island (or Looe Island) **30** comes into view ahead, one of the few inhabited islands (apart from the Isles of Scilly) off the Cornish coast. In the Middle Ages the island was always called after St Michael, but in the 17th century it began to be called St George's Island, perhaps in error! Now it is usually known as Looe Island.

From the headland a link path goes inland to the National Trust car park near Hendersick Farm. The Coast Path now hugs the coastline all the way to Hannafore, the first bit of built-up Looe that you reach. In the last field before the houses note the wreck post, just before the gate. Note also the ancient wall forming the field boundary of the first house, perhaps significantly called Monks House. Two splayed windows and some square holes look enigmatically westwards.

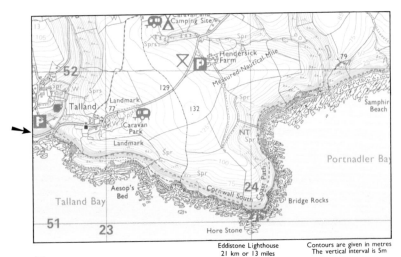

Eddistone Lighthouse
21 km or 13 miles

Contours are given in metres
The vertical interval is 5m

Having reached the road, the bridge between West and East Looe is still 1 mile (1.6 km) away, but the walk is not hard. A grass strip beside the pavement helps ease tired muscles, and there are opportunities for refreshment and much to see, as boats pass in and out of the harbour. In the main holiday season a ferry shuttles pedestrians across the harbour, which saves a few hundred yards' walk to the bridge further north.

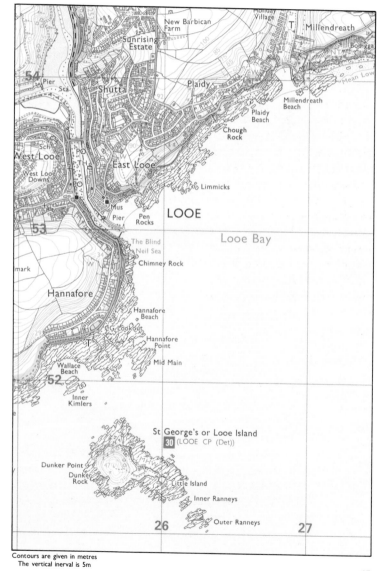

Contours are given in metres
The vertical inerval is 5m

5 Looe to Cremyll

via Portwrinkle and Mount Edgcumbe Country Park
20½ miles (33.1 km)

This is a lengthy section of the Coast Path, good in parts. Some unusual stretches of woodland walking and roadside rambling end with a stroll through a country park.

The most difficult route-finding problems occur when the walker is leaving a town. In the old part of Looe, opposite the Salutation Inn, walk up Castle Street to an open area at the top. This spot may also be reached by a zigzag path and steps from the sea wall behind East Looe Beach.

The Coast Path leaving Looe is initially on tarmac, but soon becomes a dirt track and passes along a scrubby hillside. When a road is reached, turn down Plaidy Lane. As you descend you will have a good view of fulmars perched on an outcrop to the right (south).

Plaidy Beach is a small shingle strand with a seasonal café behind a stepped concrete sea wall. The road, along which the Coast Path is routed, leads eastwards with houses on both sides. The path turns sharp right, up a steep, signposted, tarmac path, opposite a house with a steeply pitched roof. It passes through a small parking area, along a level road and, where this bends left, the Coast Path descends between two houses at a waymarked junction. The path leads down to the hubbub of Millendreath and emerges from behind Neptune's Restaurant. The valley is totally given over to holiday enjoyment.

From the east end of Millendreath Beach the Coast Path is signposted up a lane past a number of houses. Ignore the path shown on the map going through Bodigga Cliff. Landslips have made this impossible to maintain. Continue up the lane after the last of the houses where the tarmac ends. This is an attractive lane of the kind which must have served countless Cornish coves 100 years ago. This one has never been 'improved'.

When the path reaches a tarmac road at Bodigga **31** look out for a stile on the right (south side) with a doggie gate after about 150 yards (135 metres). A National Trust omega sign reads 'Bodigga Cliff'. Now you leave the road for about 1½ miles (2.4 km), and after descending rough land the path enters woods through which it undulates for some distance. Two minor paths, one up and one down, should be ignored, but the

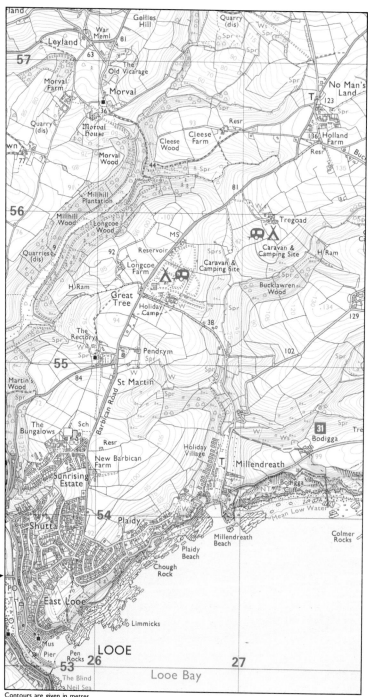

Contours are given in metres
The vertical interval is 5m

67

Coast Path is unmistakeable. Exotic shrieks and screams from the left probably come from the Monkey Sanctuary.

Emerging from the woodland, the path slants up an open stretch of scrubby land before descending to the road west of Seaton, down a flight of steps 200 yards (180 metres) west of the last bungalow on the south side of the road.

Eastwards from here there is a choice. You can follow the road for over a mile to the hairpin bend east of Downderry, or walk the concrete sea wall and then the beach, which is the route I will describe. The shoreline route is usually possible, except when a gale is blowing and the tide is high. It would then be imprudent to attempt it, and you should take the road. Walk east along the sea wall, and where this ends take to the beach. Go past the drawn-up boats to where a small stream reaches the beach, then up the path between the stream and a bungalow. The road is reached by a school, shop, garage and church **A**.

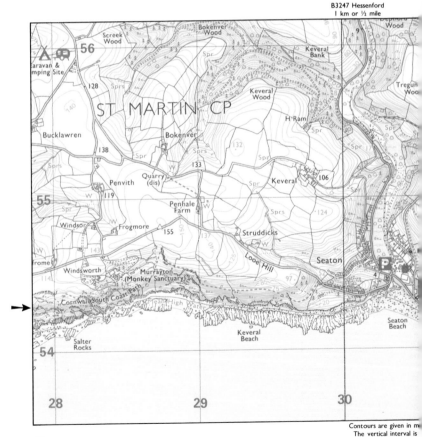

Contours are given in m
The vertical interval is

Downderry is a stretched-out village about a mile long, with modern houses at the east end. The older core is pleasant enough, and here there are shops, pubs, cafés and a Post Office. On the beach you may see the distinctive inshore crabbers drawn up. They have a small mizzen mast offset to the port side.

Perhaps surprisingly, the highest points on the south coast of Cornwall are on either side of Downderry. To the east, the Coast Path ascends to Battern Cliffs (462 feet/141 metres). To the west, although the path does not climb that far, the road between Seaton and Bodigga reaches 508 feet (155 metres).

Turn right (east) along the road to a point round the first hairpin bend where the Coast Path is signposted to the right. The path is steep in places and zigzags about, but is well cared for. It reaches a field at a stile and, in the absence of a sign, some walkers follow the lower edge of the field eastwards, but the true route is along the top hedge.

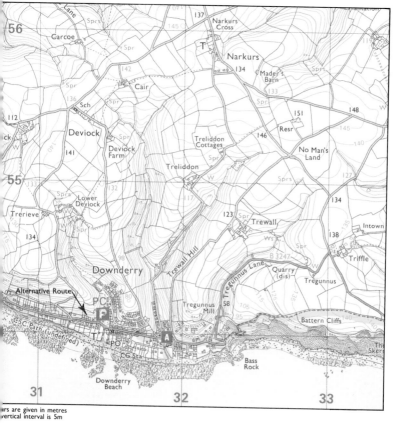

ars are given in metres
vertical interval is 5m

Where this hedge converges with the road, by a large overgrown barrow, the official Coast Path is routed along the road for just over 1 mile (1.6 km) to the lane above Portwrinkle, then down the lane to this small fishing village.

This stretch of path is the most unsatisfactory section in South Cornwall from the point of view of an established route. As the map shows, from where the path is officially routed on to the road, an *ad hoc* path, marked on the map as 'CSC path – undefined' has developed nearer the coast, and a designated right of way exists for the last third of a mile west of Portwrinkle. It is to be hoped that this unfortunate state of affairs will soon be resolved.

Portwrinkle **32** possesses a charm that is lacking in Seaton and Downderry, but it has to be admitted that the broad sweep of Whitsand Bay overpowers the settlements along its shores. The village came into existence as a pilchard fishery, and the large (for such a small place) cellars stand at the top of the slip above the harbour. On the hillside to the west of the village are two white-painted stone plinths, each with a recess on the seaward side, where fires were lit in order to guide boats back to Portwrinkle after dark.

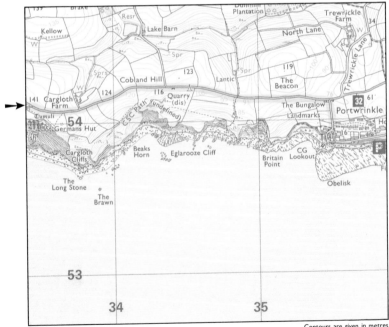

Contours are given in metres
The vertical interval is 5m

Walk east along the road from Portwrinkle harbour past the car park, ignoring a path down to the beach. The Coast Path leaves the road opposite the entrance to the Whitsand Bay Hotel **B**. Finnygook Lane leads up to Crafthole, where there is a shop, post office and the Finnygook Inn. As you climb you will see a 14th century pigeon house, a round grey stone building, on the golf course to the west.

The narrow path climbs steeply to the golf course. It follows an obvious route along the edge of the links, confirmed by the occasional signpost. The path then enters National Trust land known as Trethill Cliffs, and after a level stretch it dips steeply and climbs past a Ministry of Defence warning sign. The Tregantle firing ranges are nearby. A stile is climbed, a field edge followed, and then the road is joined at the eastern end of Trethill Cliffs.

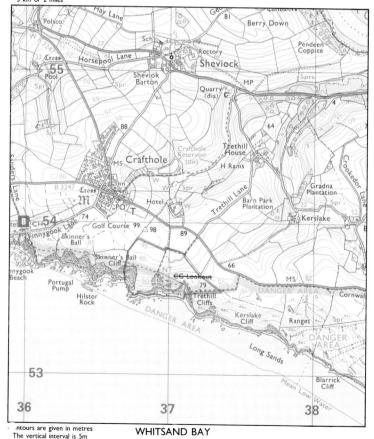

A374 Polbathic
3 km or 2 miles

Contours are given in metres
The vertical interval is 5m

WHITSAND BAY

From this point for 4 miles (6.4 km) the Coast Path follows the road, although this is not as bad as it sounds. For about half a mile (800 metres) the path is over the hedge from the road, and it is then possible to walk on a wide grass verge where it goes inland round Tregantle Fort **33** (see page 81).

Tregantle Fort is still occupied by the Ministry of Defence because of the firing ranges between the road and the sea. The firing programme for the following week is published in *The Western Morning News* on Fridays.

Just past the entrance to Tregantle Fort the road returns to the coast at Tregantle Down, and here a path descends to the beach, which can be used when firing is not taking place. A stretch of land called Tregantle Cliffs, between the road and the shore, is protected by the National Trust, but is so narrow that the Coast Path cannot be routed along it, except on the roadside bank.

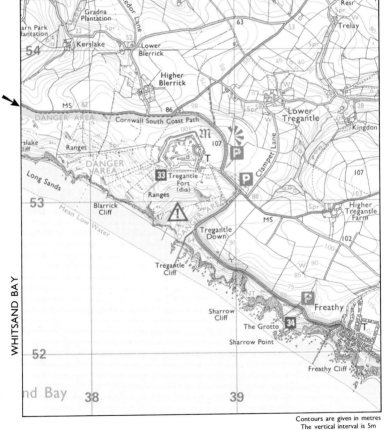

Contours are given in metres
The vertical interval is 5m

Looking east to Rame Head along Whitsand Bay from Sharrow Point.

Nearly at Freathy there is a large car park to the north of the road, and a sign on the south of the road indicates Sharrow Point. A path goes down here to Sharrow Grotto **34**, almost at sea level, and a short digression is worth the effort involved to take it. The Grotto is an artificial cave, hacked out of the cliff by a naval lieutenant called Lugger in 1784 as a therapy for his gout.

East of here there is a change of land ownership and Freathy is reached. For the next 2 miles (3.2 km), the Military Road **35** passes above a cliff peppered with huts, shacks and chalets dating back to the early 1930s. There are occasional seasonal cafés, but no opportunity to leave the road until the turning to Whitsand Bay Holiday Park is reached **C**. At low tide, when firing is not taking place, the sandy beach could be followed from beneath Tregantle Fort to Wiggle Cliff, about 3 miles (4.8 km) of walking.

At the Holiday Park junction **C**, where there is a postbox and a old War Department boundary stone, a path goes down to the Clifftop and Eddystone Cafés. Do not take this path. Instead, take the path slanting down the cliff slope on a line with the pyramid of Rame Head. In 1988 the path was not signposted where it leaves the road, but there were waymark posts along the way, past a small community of about ten huts in a combe on the cliffs. From here a path descends to the beach, but the Coast Path climbs steeply towards the road. When about 5 yards (4.5 metres) short of the road, turn off right (south) and follow this further loop path. (This is just east of Rame View and the Cabin Café and Restaurant.) Again, this was not signposted, but waymark posts are in position along the path.

Not far down, you pass a seat dedicated to Bill Best Harris, one-time Plymouth City Librarian, broadcaster and local author 'who loved these cliffs'. Just past his seat, turn up left, ignoring the path to the beach. The Coast Path undulates along and almost reaches the road near the junction to Wiggle. It then descends once more, bearing left and leaving the huts behind, passes a shuttered lean-to building, and carries on across rough ground to a stile at the far end. A private drive is followed, then the path goes behind a line of old coastguard cottages and up two flights of steps to reach another path coming down from the road near Rame. The one-time Polhawn Fort **36** is just below.

The way ahead is now clear, and this is the beginning of a circuit of Rame Head. The walking is easy, and at first there is a hedge (in Cornwall a hedge is a wall!) which displays a fine variety of plants in the summer, then the path negotiates a rocky spine. Rame Head is now quite close and worth a visit.

No walker should be surprised to find the obligatory ditch and bank across the narrow isthmus, making Rame Head defensible in Iron Age times. Practically every similar headland in Devon and Cornwall was so used. The sturdy chapel has embellished Rame Head for about 600 years, and has thus lasted far beyond the temporary structures which were raised for hostilities only during the two World Wars.

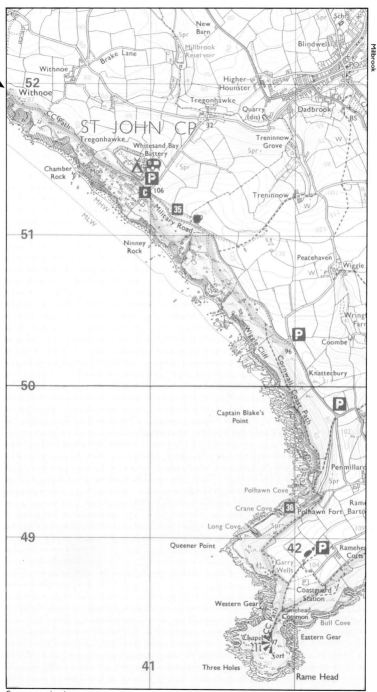

Contours are given in metres
The vertical interval is 5m

From the neck of Rame Head, ignore a lower path and follow the signposted route ascending to a wall corner. At Homebarton Hill a link path crosses a field to Rame Church, and half a mile (800 metres) further on another link path goes up to a car park on the site of the one-time Penlee Battery. When the path reaches a tarmac loop, take the lower option, which leads to a turning area and seats at Penlee Point **37**, where the Coast Path turns north and joins the Earl's Drive through sycamore woodland. Just after a quarry left and a seat right, bear downhill along a signposted path. This emerges on a road again behind the coastguard cottages, then continues to contour while the road climbs. The way ahead to Cawsand is now clear, and the Coast Path descends into the village by Pier Lane. Cawsand and Kingsand have coalesced into one place, although they retain their separate identities.

These twin villages represent the archetypal Cornish coastal settlement. Until 1844, Kingsand was in Devon and Cawsand in Cornwall, an anomalous situation which led to rivalry. In the summer it is possible to reach Plymouth quickly from Cawsand by catching one of the regular sailings from the beach to Mayflower Steps, but this would mean missing the scenic delights of Mount Edgcumbe Country Park. Cawsand is linked

The Square, Cawsand, with the fountain in the foreground.

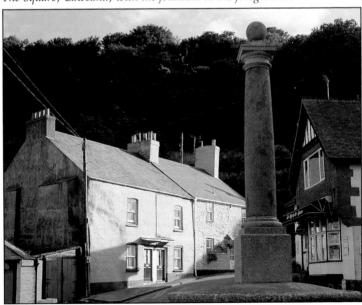

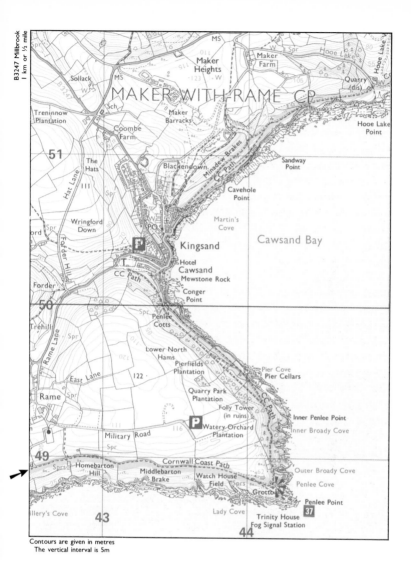

Contours are given in metres
The vertical interval is 5m

to Kingsand by Garrett Street, a narrow lane passable by vehicles only from north to south, and once in Kingsand the way out of the village is to turn up Market Street (do not follow the waterfront), then Heavitree Road. Opposite Lower Row enter Mount Edgcumbe Country Park, here a recreational area with a striking view of Plymouth Sound. The Coast Path contours this field at two levels. From the higher option a path climbs steeply to the site of the batteries on Maker Heights. The path then enters a wood of evergreen oaks called Dark Trees.

At Hooe Lake the path meets the public road leading to Picklecombe Fort, now a complex of desirable apartments, and after 50 yards (45 metres) the route turns left and you pass over a stile then walk parallel to the road. When above the fort buildings the Coast Path turns through 90 degrees 'inland' – this is the Earl's Drive once again – and where it returns to the sea you will see a feature on the bend call Picklecombe Seat. The stonework for this late 18th century conceit came from a church in Stonehouse, Plymouth.

Around the next bend, a left-hander, you go through an arch, and 60 yards (55 metres) beyond this the Coast Path descends towards the sea, down a slope shaded with rhododendrons. It zigzags down then forks right, to the cliff edge. The path drops further to a pebble beach below an isolated house. From here Drake's Island **38** appears very close. At low tide the reef known as the Bridge reaches out from the land and the island. The deep-water channel is on the east side of the island.

Beyond the beach, the path climbs through open woodland and enters a deer enclosure, so be sure to close the gate. At this spot look up left to see the ruin known simply as the Folly **39**. This is one of a number of landscape features built by the Mount Edgcumbe family to enliven their estate, and we are fortunate that this large area, so near to Plymouth, is now open to the public as a country park.

The path descends to the amphitheatre where a temple overlooks a lake with ducks, surrounded by lawns. Carrying on, you pass a boulder-built grotto, then a beach, Barn Pool, used as a tank embarkation site for the invasion of northern France in the Second World War. The path now reaches more formal gardens, with a 1540 fort on the left and a later battery on the right, complete with a mounted French 8-pounder cannon.

The Orangery, where refreshments are served, is reached, and the entrance/exit of the country park is situated nearby. The visitor centre is worth a visit and maybe, if time allows, you might look over Mount Edgcumbe House on the hill. Unfortunately the house, dating from 1540, was destroyed by fire in 1941, but the ruins were well restored. The estate, which takes in much of the coastline round to Whitsand Bay, became a country park in 1970. Leaflets and other publications are on sale in the visitor centre, and guided walks are undertaken by the Ranger Service.

The ferry leaves this point – Cremyll – for Stonehouse on the other side at fairly frequent intervals (see page 158).

At the time of writing there is no recognised route through Plymouth for the walker. If you intend to pick up the Coast Path beyond, at Turnchapel, you must either walk – a lengthy undertaking – or ride by taxi or bus. (There is no ferry across the Cattewater to Turnchapel, despite what old maps might show.) Buses do run but, in these days of transport deregulation, what applies today may not do so tomorrow, so I can only suggest you enquire locally.

Plymouth Youth Hostel is at Belmont Place, Devonport Road, Stoke, Plymouth. As you pass through the town, at least find time to visit Royal Parade, the Hoe and what is called the Barbican – the area fronting the west side of Sutton Harbour.

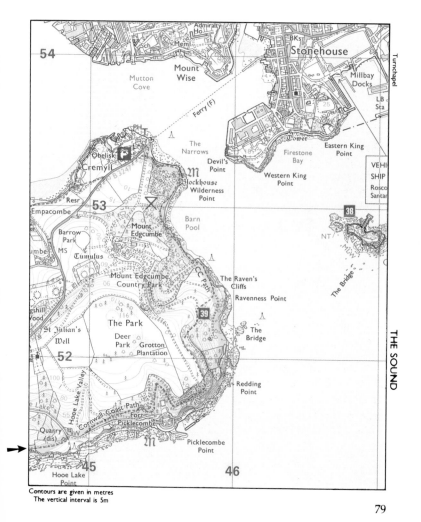

Contours are given in metres
The vertical interval is 5m

A CIRCULAR WALK ROUND RAME HEAD

5 miles (7.9 km)

From the public car park on Rame Head beyond Rame Church, walk out to Rame Head itself. Now follow the Coast Path anticlockwise round Penlee Point **37** and on to Cawsand. In Cawsand, having explored the village and, if time allows, Kingsand as well, walk up Rame Lane, past Rame Barton and descend the lane to meet the Coast Path above Polhawn Fort **36**. Finally, follow the path around to Rame Head and return to the car park.

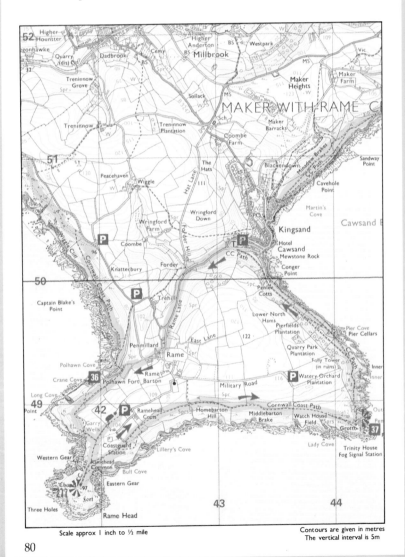

Scale approx 1 inch to ½ mile

Contours are given in metres
The vertical interval is 5m

Tregantle Fort

This massive structure **33** is one of about 40 forts and batteries built in the 1860s and early 1870s to protect Plymouth and its dockyard from the perceived threat of French ambitions and newly developed sea power. The first French iron-clad *La Gloire* was laid down in 1858, so Lord Palmerston set up a Royal Commission in 1859 'to consider the defences of the United Kingdom'. The name 'Palmerston Follies' has been ascribed to them.

Penlee Point

Penlee Point **37** is an important feature on the Coast Path, for here the path changes direction and Plymouth comes into view. The 1827 grotto just below the path is known as Adelaide's 'chapel', though it never had pretensions to sanctity. The Earl of Mount Edgcumbe had the Earl's Drive built out to Penlee Point – you come across it again in Mount Edgcumbe Country Park – and had the grotto built in honour of Princess Adelaide, the wife of Prince William (later King William IV) who stayed at Mount Edgcumbe and enjoyed visiting Penlee.

The Folly in Mount Edgcumbe Country Park. Plymouth and Drake's Island lie beyond.

6 Turnchapel to Mothecombe

via Warren Point and along Revelstoke Drive
15 miles (24.3 km)

Turnchapel **40** is an inconvenient place for the next length of Coast Path to start from! So near, but yet so far, it is only a short distance across the Cattewater from Cattedown on the Plymouth side, but the lack of a ferry to get there means a detour of several miles round Laira Bridge. Even a die-hard Plymothian would be hard-pressed to say anything in favour of a pedestrian stroll from Plymouth city centre to Turnchapel, so, until the waterfront is improved or the ferry reinstated, I would suggest a bus, a taxi or a friend's car as being the best way to reach the start of the South Devon Coast Path. I will assume you have reached Turnchapel, and take it from there.

The purist may want to commence walking the Coast Path from the water's edge. A 300-yard (275-metre) walk downhill from the bus terminus at the RAF Mountbatten guardroom brings you to the old ferry slip where a sign announces 'Free Public Landing'.

Turnchapel **40** is a pleasant backwater, largely given over to marine repairs, but with little to detain you unless it be the Boringdon Arms or the New Inn. Climb the hill from the waterfront and on the wall corner opposite RAF Mountbatten guardroom note the plaque which states that T. E. Lawrence (Lawrence of Arabia, 1888–1935) was stationed here in the flying boat squadron from 1929 to 1935. He was then known as Shaw. The Ministry of Defence announced in April 1989 that this station is to close in the mid-1990s.

At the top of the hill, turn right (west) at the T-junction. The massive walls here belong to another Palmerston fort; this one was Fort Stamford, and is now a leisure centre. Where the road bears left (south), carry straight on with a fence left, bearing round into an open public space. This is Jennycliff, a popular viewpoint, but the walker may well be spurred on to less popular clifftops.

The Coast Path follows the top edge of Jennycliff Field, getting up on to the road at the southern end, and uses the road (mind the traffic!) for a few hundred yards until, where the road bears inland at a small combe, the Coast Path peels off on the downslope side. This is a most attractive length of path. Good views to the right, and a feeling of relief at having got away from

Contours are given in metres
The vertical interval is 5m

people and traffic, put bounce into the walker's stride. Soon Plymouth Breakwater **41** comes into view, and on the inland side the enormous brick wall is the back stop of a firing range.

Fort Bovisand and harbour **42** lie just below. The harbour was built between 1816 and 1824, initially to enable ships to take on fresh water without having to go up to the dockyard. A reservoir was constructed in the valley behind Bovisand Bay, and the water piped to the ships.

The Coast Path descends behind Fort Bovisand **42**, bears left, and crosses a deep ravine by a footbridge. This artificial cutting was excavated to enable ammunition and supplies to be transported to the fort below. A further drop **A** brings you down between two rows of cottages, the westerly being the older terrace. The path now passes behind Bovisand Bay, where much building has taken place in recent years. Some, it has to be said, replaces ramshackle huts and chalets from pre-war days.

Once past Andurn Point you can enjoy three-quarters of a mile (1.2 km) of pleasant easy rambling along low cliffs almost at sea level. Although only $2\frac{1}{2}$ miles (4 km) has been covered since leaving Turnchapel, several different types of rock have been traversed. Turnchapel is on Plymouth limestone, Jennycliff on tuffs, abreast of Staddon Heights there were grits and shales, and there is slate at Bovisand. South of Andurn Point the low cliffs bear deposits of head, a matrix of rock waste formed in Ice Age times by alternate freezing and thawing. This is a conglomerate material brought down from higher levels when

Fort Bovisand, now a training school for underwater activities.

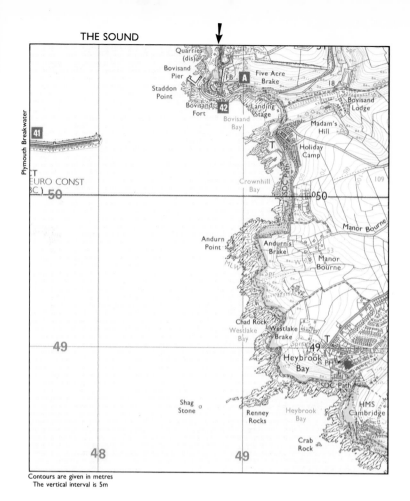

Contours are given in metres
The vertical interval is 5m

colder conditions prevailed. The transition from one geological structure to another is typical of the South Devon coast.

The Coast Path now enters, and just as rapidly leaves, Heybrook Bay, a bit of Plymouth suburbia-by-the-sea. Once over the stream you will see a warning sign for firing ranges – you have reached HMS *Cambridge*, the Royal Navy gunnery school at Wembury Point, but if no firing is taking place you can carry on along the Coast Path, almost within touching distance of the guns. If firing is scheduled there is a signposted route through the establishment, but be prepared for gunfire noise. (Similar notices warn walkers approaching from the east.) Clearly, it is unwise to picnic or hang about in front of the guns. There are proposals at the time of writing to erect a high security fence around the camp.

As you pass HMS *Cambridge* you are as near the Great Mew Stone **43** as you will get. This is one of several similarly named rocks along the south coast, and the largest. 'Mew' is an old name for gull.

The Coast Path to Wembury Beach is easily followed as it traces the low cliff edge. An earlier cliff line in geological time is visible one field back from the present shore. This is a feature you will see again further east. A one-time water mill is now a seasonal café run by the National Trust, and a National Trust shop is situated in a separate building nearby. The toilets are managed by the local authority. On the hill above the large car park is Wembury Church **44**, so conspicuously sited that it must have been built here as a landmark for shipping.

The Coast Path climbs eastwards from just above the café, and in the summer a notice at the path take-off point informs walkers of the ferry times, as $1\frac{1}{2}$ miles (2.4 km) further on the deep water at the mouth of the River Yealm (pronounced 'Yam') has to be crossed, and the operating times of the ferry are limited (see pages 158–9).

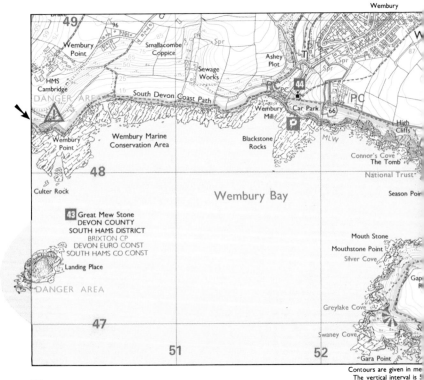

Contours are given in me
The vertical interval is 5

The path to the Yealm is a high-level one with fine views ahead. National Trust land is soon entered, and the path is mostly within Trust ownership until Stoke Point is reached 6 miles (9.6 km) ahead. At the Rocket House **B**, where coastguard apparatus used to be stored, there is a choice of route: down the vehicle track to the right, or straight on along the high-level path. The latter is scenically more attractive, as just before the path drops to the Yealm the view up the creeks past Newton Ferrers with Dartmoor in the distance will make you pause.

The descent is steep and brings you to the ferry point. Provided the ferry is running it can be hailed from here. It is suggested that if journeying from east to west, you should turn left (west) on landing on the north shore of the Yealm and walk up to Rocket House **B** the easy way.

When you land on the Noss Mayo side, note the restored ferryman's sign exhibited there. Part of it reads: 'Ferriage for every person on weekdays 1d; the like on Sundays 2d. For every pony and ass 3d.'

Now turn right (west) along a narrow path that climbs through oak woods in which the invasive rhododendron is beginning to take hold. The path meets a wide drive just short of a gate where there is a National Trust interpretive panel. Beyond the gate the drive continues round a bend at Battery Cottage, a sprawling country house on a one-time gun position.

ours are given in metres
vertical interval is 5m

On the seaward side, a path cuts down to Cellar Beach, a west-facing but usually sheltered cove. A row of coastguard cottages is passed. You now turn your back on houses – with one exception – for several miles, for this is the Revelstoke Drive **45**, a carefully engineered route round the cliffs which the Coast Path follows as far as Beacon Hill. Lord Revelstoke, whose home was at Membland, east of Noss Mayo, had this carriage drive cut in the 19th century by local fishermen. It encircled his property, and enabled him to impress his guests as he showed off his land. It makes an excellent high-level walking route.

The Coast Path enters Brakehill Plantation, and emerging at the west end, bears left and left again round first Mouthstone Point and then Gara Point. This is wonderful walking. The path is level and well surfaced, the views are magnificent, and in summer the gently sloping pasture between the path and the sea is a favoured habitat for birds, flowers and butterflies. These slopes are fenced off into large compartments for the better management of sheep flocks, and walkers must keep their dogs on leads. Cases of sheep being frightened over cliffs are not unknown.

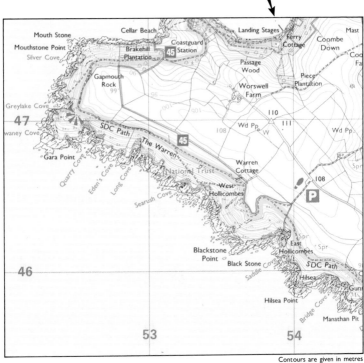

Contours are given in metres
The vertical interval is 5m

This stretch is known as the Warren, as in the 19th century it was managed for the propagation of rabbits. Warren Cottage, with its massive gateposts, is passed on the lower side. These distinctive gateposts are a feature of the South Hams, as this part of Devon, between Dartmoor and the English Channel, is known. Warren Cottage was built for the warrener who farmed the rabbits that bred on the cliffs.

Once round Blackstone Point a link path goes inland a few hundred yards to a National Trust car park, but the Coast Path continues eastwards, passing the disused Gunrow Signal Station. Buried nearby in the turf are the concrete bases of Second World War structures. Just west of Stoke Point another link path heads north to a recently built car park, and then, having turned Stoke Point, the path leaves National Trust land and passes along a narrow vegetated section, although Revelstoke Drive **45** is still there beneath your feet.

A road and a car park are reached at Stoke House, and a small shop 50 yards (45 metres) below the car park is open from 1 April to the end of October, primarily for people using the caravan site but useful for walkers, too. The road leads down to the caravan site and the ruined and tucked-away church of St Peter the Poor Fisherman **46**. The diversion means a steep climb back again, but the experience repays the effort.

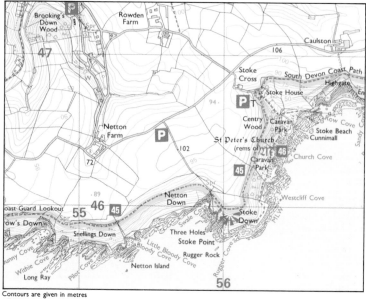

Contours are given in metres
The vertical interval is 5m

Now continue eastwards on the drive, here a terrace on the hillside, and in places rather poached by cattle. A view back reveals the caravan site and the church for those who did not go down the hill. The view ahead now includes Burgh Island, which is visited in the next chapter.

Where the Revelstoke Drive **45** turns inland at Beacon Hill a ruined folly built of stone with brick detailing is passed. This prominent feature is shown as Membland Pleasure House on Donn's map of 1765. The Coast Path here asserts itself once more and, freed from the shackles of the Revelstoke Drive, plunges down to join a track visible ahead. This is possibly the steepest haul on the whole of the path, and is as unpleasant in descending as in ascending.

Where the farm track turns inland the Coast Path carries straight on, and is well waymarked through a succession of fields. St Anchorite's Rock beckons as a prominent feature on the coastline. However, a descent has to be negotiated first to the sheltered valley below Carswell, a verdant glen with its own little crag, Saddle Rock. St Anchorite's Rock is then reached, but disappoints on close acquaintance. It looks more impressive from a distance.

Heading eastwards, the Coast Path follows the hedge to a double stile. The next field is crossed, then the path bears right,

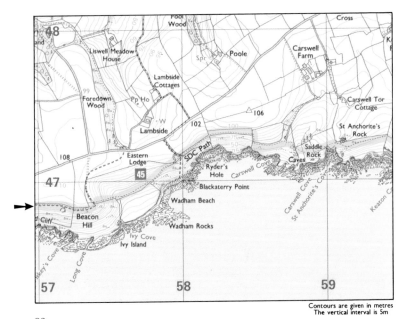

Contours are given in metres
The vertical interval is 5m

towards the cliff, and follows the edge down to Butcher's Cove where a cutting through the rock tells of farmers' forays to get sand and seaweed for the land. The path descends to sea level at Bugle Hole, then climbs steeply up a well-planned zigzag.

The path now traces the field edges right (east), enters woods, and drops down to Meadowsfoot (or Mothecombe) Beach. This beach is open to the public only on Wednesdays, Saturdays and Sundays, but walkers may follow the path to the far side of the beach where it strikes up through the woods of Owen's Hill, and down the other side to meet the road to the slipway and the ford across the mouth of the Erme.

Mothecombe is the hamlet near the car park, and is part of the Flete Estate through whose benign ownership the whole of this beautiful estuary has retained its tranquil atmosphere. The few houses, and the old coastguard cottages near the slipway, are the only dwellings, and no new buildings have been erected this century. The old school is open for refreshments in the summer. The two slipways and the Coast Path apart, there is no public access to the estuary.

For the walker intending to cross to the east bank there is only one way – it has to be waded. The alternative is a 9-mile (14.4-km) diversion inland round Sequers Bridge (before fording, see page 159).

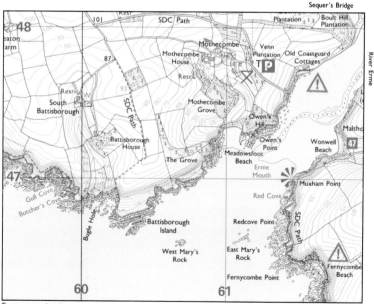

Contours are given in metres
The vertical interval is 5m

A circular walk round the Revelstoke Drive at the mouth of the Yealm

4¼ miles (6.8 km)

From the National Trust's Warren Cliffs car park, pass out of the entrance, turn left and then right after 35 yards (32 metres) down an unmade road. This leads to Noss Mayo, an attractive village facing the larger settlement of Newton Ferrers across the tidal creek. Turn left opposite Noss Mayo car park, then right along a narrow road. After the last cottage on the left ascend the steps on the left, near a National Trust sign, into Fordhill Plantation. This path takes the walker off a narrow road, and should be followed to its end. Where the path rejoins the road (grid ref. 540476) – here the Revelstoke Drive **45** – turn right, and left after 25 yards (23 metres), to the ferry slip. Continue along a narrow path, through oak woods to a wide drive. Once through the gate the drive passes Battery Cottage, a country house, then enters Brakehill Plantation. When out of the trees, bear left around Mouthstone Point, then left again around Gara Point. Walk along the Warren, past Warren Cottage to Blackstone Point. Once past Blackstone Point, follow the link path inland back to the car park.

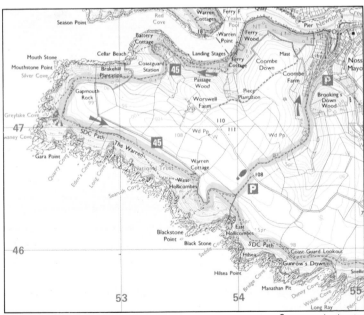

Contours are given in metres
The vertical interval is 5m

Noss Mayo in the foreground, with Newton Ferrers in the background, at high tide.

Wembury Marine Conservation Area

Wembury Point is about halfway along the Wembury Marine Conservation Area, which stretches from Fort Bovisand to Gara Point, the headland to the east of the Great Mew Stone. Visitors are asked not to interfere with the marine life, which is rich in the shallow waters off the coast from Bovisand Bay to the mouth of the Yealm and was so threatened by recreational and educational activities that the whole area was designated a Marine Conservation Area. Leaflets explaining the designation can be obtained from the National Trust café at Wembury, the Fort Bovisand Underwater Centre and Plymouth City Museum (Natural History Department).

7 Wonwell to Salcombe

across the Avon Estuary
18½ miles (29.5 km)

The east side of the Erme Estuary is even less populated than the west side and the narrow approach lane to the slipway gives few opportunities for parking. Drivers must not obstruct the highway. The only pedestrian way across to the west side is to wade at low tide (see page 159).

Near the top of the east bank slipway a sign reads 'Coast Path Crossing Point 230m at Low Tide', and an arrow points out the direction. Opposite this notice a footpath sign indicates the Coast Path, and up a few steps the route goes into Wrinkle Wood and south along the side of the estuary. Leaving the wood, the fenced path continues to Wonwell Beach, where the ruins include a one-time pilot house **47**. Before the estuary silted up, small coasting vessels crept upriver with cargoes of limestone and coal for the lime kilns, and they needed a pilot to guide them past the constantly changing sand banks; the pilot lived in this cottage. You will notice that some embryo sand dunes are trying to establish themselves here. Up the side valley you can see the clogged ditches of water meadows when the light is right. Water was channelled along these carefully cut, gently descending leats, and when extra irrigation was required to provide an early bite, the banks were broken down and the water allowed to flow across the hillside. The indistinct lines of such ditches can be seen in many places in Devon, pointing to an agricultural practice now absent from the country calendar.

Muxham Point gives a superb view up the Erme, and there are some small rocky outcrops that provide good shelter for a picnic. The path is now clear all the way to Bigbury-on-Sea, and lies mostly between the cliff edge and the field fence. It is, however, a very strenuous stretch of the route, with severe undulations between Freshwater and Challaborough. Signs pointing in both directions warn of holes in the Coast Path caused by animals.

The first cove you meet is Westcombe Beach **A** and here a sign provided by the South Devon Heritage Coast Service points to a route up the valley to Kingston. The building that you see here was a stable block for the horses when the Mildmay family, which has owned all the land fringeing the Erme Estuary for over a century, came for picnics.

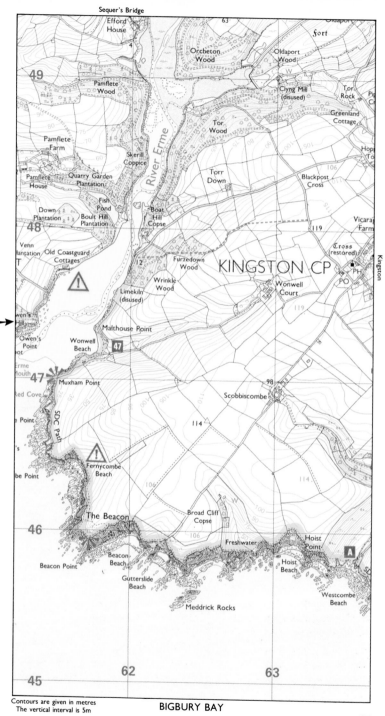

Sequer's Bridge

Efford
House

Orcheton
Wood

Oldaport
fort

Oldaport
Wood

Pamflete
Wood

Clyng Mill
(disused)

Tor
Rock

49

Greenland
Cottage

Pamflete
Farm

Skerill
Coppice

Tor
Wood

Hop
To

Pamflete
House

Quarry Garden
Plantation

Torr
Down

Blackpost
Cross

106

Down
Plantation

Boult Hill
Plantation

Fish
Pond

Boat
Hill
Copse

Vicara
Farm

48

119

Venn
lantation

Old Coastguard
Cottages

Furzedown
Wood

KINGSTON CP

Cross
(restored)

PH
PO

Kingston

⚠

Wrinkle
Wood

Limekiln
(disused)

Wonwell
Court

wen's
ill

Malthouse Point

119

Owen's
Point
ot

Wonwell
Beach

47

rme
outh

47

Muxham Point

98

Red Cove

Scobbiscombe

Point

SDC Path

114

⚠

Fernycombe
Beach

114

e Point

106

The Beacon

Broad Cliff
Copse

46

Freshwater

Hoist
Point

A

Beacon
Beach

Hoist
Beach

Beacon Point

Gutterslide
Beach

Westcombe
Beach

Meddrick Rocks

62

63

45

Contours are given in metres
The vertical interval is 5m

BIGBURY BAY

95

After a climb, descend to Ayrmer Cove where two paths head inland to Ringmore. This is the village where R. C. Sherriff wrote *Journey's End*, his play about the First World War, and the pub is named after it. Over the next hill and down the other side is the expansive family holiday village of Challaborough – by a topographical trick not noticed from the west until one is almost there. The Coast Path goes round the back of the beach and on to Bigbury-on-Sea; another popular holiday resort with masses of sand. Youth hostellers are warned that the hostel which used to operate here was closed not long ago.

If time allows, the walker should stroll across the sands to Burgh Island **48**. Even if the tide is in, the island may still be reached for a few pence by using the sea tractor.

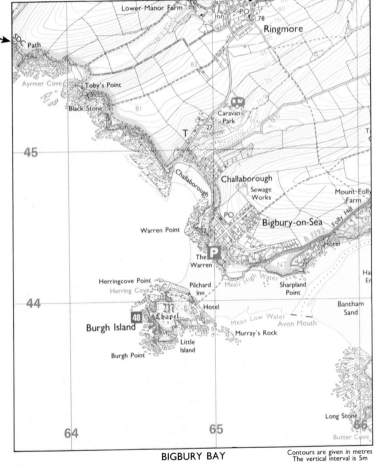

BIGBURY BAY

Contours are given in metres
The vertical interval is 5m

From Bigbury, if you are heading east, you need to cross the mouth of the Avon to reach Bantham **49** (see page 159), and if the tide is low you may walk along the sands beneath the cliffs. However, if the tide is high, or coming in, there is a risk of being cut off, and you should walk up the road – diverting briefly round the pleasant 7 acres (2.8 hectares) of the National Trust's Clematon Hill property – and go up the road to Folly Farm. Turn in where you see a sign giving the ferry times, and follow the Coast Path down to Cockleridge, an open dune-like area. The ferry crosses to Bantham from the southern tip of Cockleridge.

Having crossed, there is an opportunity to look at Bantham **49**, once something of a port, but now given over to beach fun. The area is owned by the Evans Estates. The quay at Bantham is now used only by small-boat sailors.

From the road above the ferry (south side) there is a choice of routes. You can loop round the sandspit (the Ham) or go straight on through the car park and out to the headland at the south end of Bantham Sands. Bathing can be dangerous here. Having rounded the point beyond the lifeguards' hut, the path climbs to the ridge whose western end is the Long Stone, a

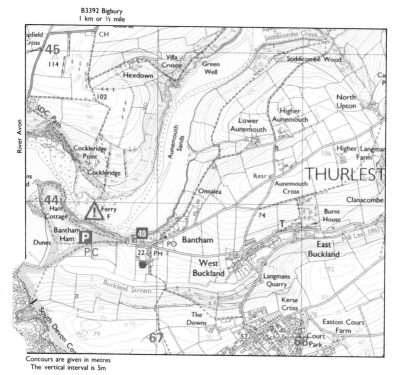

Contours are given in metres
The vertical interval is 5m

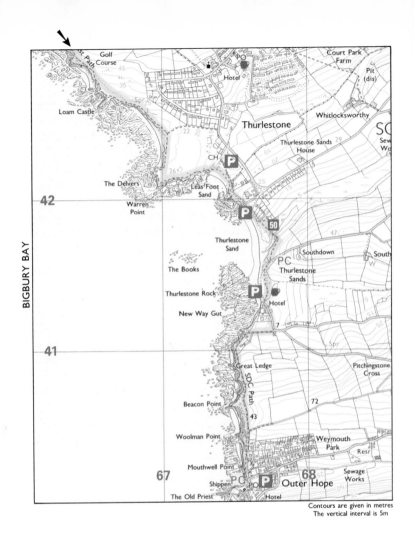

Contours are given in metres
The vertical interval is 5m

prominent seashore stack. Bolt Tail beckons a few miles ahead,
and Malborough Church spire reminds you that Salcombe is
about 2 miles (3.2 km) beyond its ancient pinnacle.

Soon you have the golf course for company. This section has a
rich variety of plants and insects. Large areas of wild white
clover, sea thrift, marguerite daisies and many other species
attract a profusion of butterflies.

Along here there is a string of sandy bays, not all of which are
named on maps. They are, from north to south, Broad Sand,
Yarner Sand, Leasfoot Sand, and Thurlestone Sand (sometimes
called South Milton Sands). Leasfoot Sand is backed by a large
car park and the club house of the golf course. The wreck lying

off it is that of the *Louis Sheid*, a famous name in South Devon lifeboat history after it went aground in December 1939, having saved 62 survivors from the Dutch passenger ship *Tajandoen*.

The Coast Path goes seaward of a large block of flats, Links Court (once the Links Hotel), passes a car park, and drops to cross South Milton Ley by an 80-yard (73-metre) footbridge. South Milton Ley **50** is the second largest reed bed in Devon, and is managed by the Devon Bird Watching and Preservation Society. The footbridge is a good place from which to observe reed and sedge warblers, moorhens and herons.

From South Milton Sands car park the Coast Path has to go slightly inland, past the Heron House Hotel, and then it returns to the coast beside the La Mer Hotel. The way is now clear due south to Outer Hope, which is coupled to its twin, Inner Hope, by a link path below the Cottage Hotel.

The Coast Path goes up from the lifeboat house at Inner Hope and out through National Trust land to Bolt Tail, which, to prevent damage to the Iron Age earthwork, should be entered by the original entrance about halfway along the embankment. Proceed to the tip of Bolt Tail. Now turn and head east, past Redrot Cove and Ramillies **51**, named after the naval ship which drove into the cliffs. Then go up the fenced-off cliff path towards Graystone with its views back to the north-west.

The path rises to Bolberry Down, where there is a large National Trust car park (the whole of the coastline from Bolt Tail to Bolt Head is owned by the National Trust).

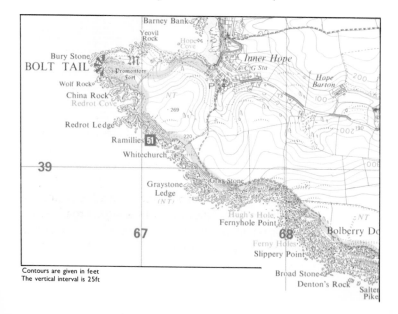

Contours are given in feet
The vertical interval is 25ft

Soar Mill Cove, looking west towards Bolberry Down.

From the east end of the Bolberry Down car park the Coast Path continues along the crest of a rocky spine, with the cliffs on one side and a sheep-grazed valley on the other. The outcrop of Hazel Tor is across the valley. One is very conscious of the rock here – it is mica schist, of a type that fractures into flat or longitudinal pieces. Slabs used to be raised on edge and made into primitive field boundaries and you can see some along here.

The Coast Path now drops down to the back of Soar Mill Cove **52**, and at the foot of the descent note the large timber gatepost. It bears an incised inscription reading 'Certified to accommodate 4 seamen' and was washed ashore in the cove some years ago. Out to sea you will notice the Ham Stone **53**, which the four-masted barque the *Herzogin Cecilie* struck in April 1936.

The beach here is attractive to bathers at certain states of the tide, but swimmers should not go out too far. The setting of the cove in a totally unspoilt situation makes it a desirable destination for those who scorn items such as deck chairs, fun floats and refreshment kiosks. Instead, its devotees make do with natural attractions, such as the spring squill that blooms here.

A climb out of the valley eastwards, keeping close to the cliffs, brings the walker up to the Warren, and there is every reason to follow the well-trodden route along the top of the cliffs, and not the public footpath shown on the map running parallel but a little inland. The views are much better, and one sees rocky outcrops, such as the Goat, which punctuate the sidelands between Steeple Cove and Off Cove.

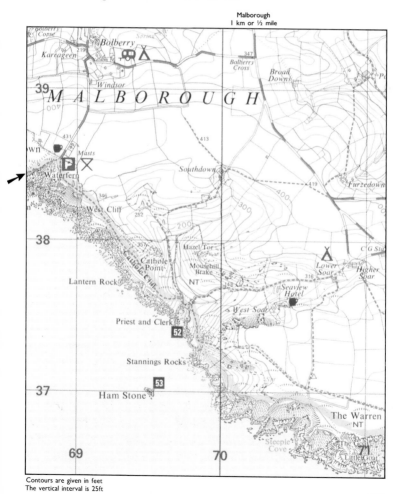

Malborough
I km or ½ mile

Contours are given in feet
The vertical interval is 25ft

Contours are given
The vertical interval

This high-level path now meets the more inland route, enters a field briefly, then leaves the field by a stile to carry on through the gorse. This leads to another stile, on the other side of which the path heads down a grassy gulley towards the knobbly point of Bolt Head. A Second World War lookout and accommodation block are built into the rocks.

From the foot of the ravine the Coast Path bears round to the north, and for the first time you can see the next stretch of coastline to be walked, from East Portlemouth to Prawle Point.

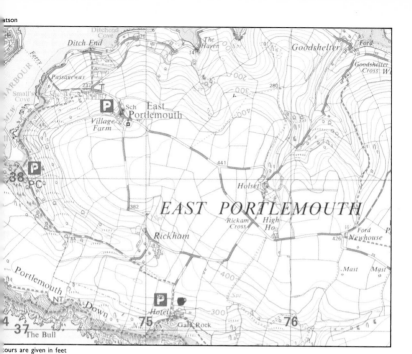

ours are given in feet
vertical interval is 25ft

The path descends to the back of Starehole Bay, then turns 90 degrees eastwards to pass round the spiky crags of Sharp Tor. This is the Courtenay Walk, a path cut by a member of the Courtenay family in the last century to give access to Bolt Head.

A straightforward walk of 2 miles (3.2 km) now brings the walker into Salcombe (see page 105), a haven for anyone interested in small boats, but the official Coast Path stops at the foot of the hill up to Overbecks **B**. This early 20th century house and 6 acres (2.4 hectares) of beautiful garden were left to the National Trust in 1937 by Mr Otto Overbeck. Much of the house is used as Salcombe Youth Hostel, and in the rest is a small museum of local bygones. The mild climate enables unusual plants to be grown. Overbecks' garden is designated a Grade II garden in the English Heritage *Register of Parks and Gardens of Special Historic Interest*.

The rest of the route to the ferry is along roads that are narrow and frequently very busy, but there is no alternative. In the summer, however, it may be worth checking to see if the occasional boat service is running between South Sands and Salcombe. This would save the last mile. For details of the ferry service to East Portlemouth, see page 159.

A circular walk around Bolt Head

4 miles (6.4 km)

From the car park at the National Trust property of Overbecks **B** at the south end of Salcombe, walk down the hill, the way you drove up, turning sharp right at the bottom. Follow the Courtenay Walk out to Sharp Tor and on to Bolt Head. From the tip of Bolt Head, walk north-west up the grassy ravine and follow the Coast Path around to the left and over a stile. The path bears right, round Off Cove, crosses another stile to enter a field, then leaves it at its south-west corner. Now follow the wall right – the Coast Path diverges away to the left – and after 500 yards (460 metres) turn right, off the open land, along a path going past the derelict buildings of Middle Soar to a road. Turn left here, then right, along a straight track beyond a gravel depot. At the end of the track turn right, then left over a stile signposted YHA and to Salcombe. This is a National Trust permissive path. Follow the path straight across several fields and stiles, then left at a path signposted to Overbecks. Walk north between a fence and hedge to a stile, where you turn right, and go down to Overbecks car park and back to the start of the walk.

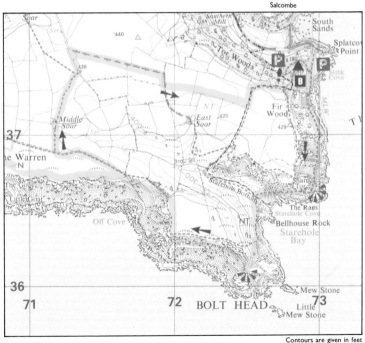

Contours are given in feet
The vertical interval is 25ft

104

Salcombe

The visitor could be excused for thinking that Salcombe has a history stretching back to ancient times, but this would be wrong. Until early last century it was East Portlemouth on the opposite shore that was the dominant settlement, and Batson, at the head of the first creek to the north of Salcombe, also has pretensions to a past. Salcombe became established as a ship-building town for the racy fruit schooners that were built along the waterfront. These speedy craft had to be capable of quick trips to bring the fruit to England in good condition from the Azores, West Indies and the Mediterranean. At the same time, early holidaymakers were coming to Devon's southernmost town for its mild climate. There is a castle here, it is true; another of those built by Henry VIII to defend the harbour and anchorage. It had to wait for action until 1643 when it came into its own during the Civil War.

Visitors now come to Salcombe in great numbers, by sea as well as by land, and the many-tentacled Kingsbridge Estuary, or Salcombe Harbour, as the different components are called, provides sheltered moorings and scope for much natural history interest. The estuary is in fact a ria, or drowned valley. No large rivers find their way into its waters, so the salinity is undiluted. At the head of the tidal waters is Kingsbridge, a busy market town, and the focus for life in this part of Devon.

Salcombe waterfront.

8 East Portlemouth to Torcross

past Prawle Point and Hallsands
12¾ miles (20.4 km)

From the ferry landing at East Portlemouth walk up to the minor road and turn right (south). In one-third of a mile (500 metres) this brings you to Mill Bay where there is a fine stretch of sand at low tide. In fact, when the tide is out there is a string of sandy coves stretching for about a mile along the east shore of Salcombe Harbour. At high tide they disappear, except for Mill Bay.

The Coast Path leaves Mill Bay by the lower path option through the woods. The higher path runs parallel and the two meet up 1½ miles (2.4 km) further on, but the lower path gives closer contact with the sea. Much of the route between here and Prawle Point is on National Trust land.

The path now heads east with the agricultural land of Portlemouth Down stretching inland from the higher path. Until the late 19th century this area was divided into hundreds of small

Disused thatched lookout, Gara Rock Hotel.

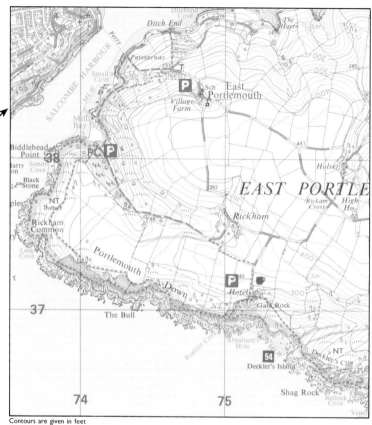

Contours are given in feet
The vertical interval is 25ft

strip fields, but these were swept away and some time later a golf course was established there, which has now also gone.

This length of path is a good place to observe the dodder, a parasitic plant displaying tiny flowers and a mass of red capillary tendrils, which seems to be suffocating its host plant, the gorse, like an all-enveloping hairnet. Kestrels and ravens are likely to be seen overhead, and shags and cormorants congregate on a shoreline rock.

Below the Gara Rock Hotel – once coastguard cottages, and still boasting a preserved thatched lookout – the lower path keeps the walker nearest the sea, and drops to Rickham Sands **54**, a pleasant place for a bathe. Decklers Cliff to the east has recently been found by the National Trust's archaeologists to have a previously unsuspected field system, possibly medieval or earlier.

Beyond Decklers Cliff a path descends to Moor Sands, an even more isolated cove than Rickham Sands. Offshore from here an 'historic wreck' has been designated **55**, which is believed to date from Bronze Age times, say 3,000 years ago at least.

For some obscure reason, a succession of place names having a porcine theme is passed – Pig's Nose, Ham Stone (another!) and Gammon Head. The name Pig's Nose is also preserved in the name of a pub in East Prawle, the inside of which is decorated with dozens of postcards depicting pigs. Gammon Head is the most distinctive headland on the south coast of Devon, a rocky spur sheltering Maceley Cove, the apotheosis of the remote sandy cove. This delectable beach can only be reached by a scramble, but the experience will not disappoint.

The Coast Path continues around the back of Elender Cove and climbs steeply abreast of Signalhouse Point to reach Devon's southernmost headland, Prawle Point **56**, by the coast-guard lookout. Signalhouse Point was bought by the National Trust in 1985. The purpose of the 'Signal House' is unknown, but the ruins of a small structure can be seen on the cliff top, and the first edition one-inch Ordnance Survey map shows a building with a track leading to it.

The map in this guide shows a number of long narrow fields between the coast and Prawle Point lane, 'behind' Signalhouse

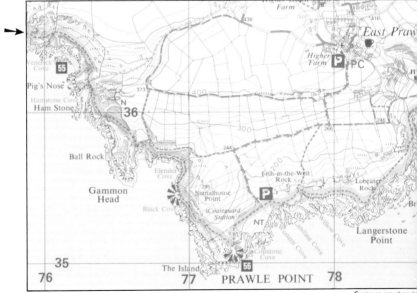

Contours are given in
The vertical interval is

Point. Unfortunately these walls were bulldozed over the cliff before coming into the Trust's ownership. The orthostat walls, made of flat upright stones set on edge, which continued these field boundaries down the sidelands, still remain.

Prawle Point means 'lookout hill', and it has been a vantage point against invaders since early times. In the First World War a hostilities-only airfield flew DH6 and DH9 aircraft from near East Prawle, and Second World War bunkers blister the little valley to the east of the point.

East from here for several miles the Coast Path follows a low, level route. A succession of fields is entered, tracing the path which is always on the seaward side of the crops. For nearly 2 miles (3.2 km), the Torrs, the early Pleistocene cliff line, rear up to your left (north). Once past the isolated Malcombe (or Maelcombe) House, which in 1988 offered accommodation, the path carries on around Woodcombe Point, and the pinnacle on its west side is worth looking out for. In the Woodcombe Valley

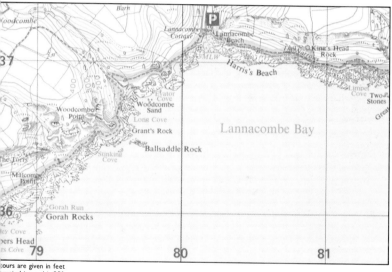

cours are given in feet
vertical interval is 25ft

a path heads inland, but the Coast Path, after dog-legging north, continues eastwards, passing a house, in front of what may have been coastguard cottages with a lookout.

Lannacombe is a popular beach in summer, and cars penetrate down the valley although space is limited. A water mill and lime kiln operated here at one time. The next stretch is due east along the Narrows to Great Mattiscombe Sand (pronounced Matchcombe), and the landmarks to look out for just west of the beach are the Pinnacles, isolated stacks of glacial head on schist bases. This is an attractive beach, although dangerous for swimming; cars cannot reach it, but there is a car park at Start Farm one-third of a mile (500 metres) north.

The Coast Path now negotiates the headland and goes on to Start Point, an exhilarating walk between frost-sculpted rock-faces on one side and disturbed sea on the other. This is a wild scene, where one feels very close to elemental forces.

Round the corner, Start Point Lighthouse **57** comes into view, a reminder of the hazards of the coast. It stands, soap-powder white, at the end of a cock's-comb ridge of schist. The name Start in this case comes from the Anglo-Saxon word *steort* meaning a tail, an element found in the name of the bird, the redstart. The lighthouse was built in 1836, and carries a fog signal.

Once again, a different view now presents itself. The gently parabolic sweep of Start Bay is lined up roughly south to north, giving a very direct route onwards. Go up the lighthouse road to the car park at Start Farm, and cross the stile opposite. There now follows a good uncomplicated path as far as Hallsands, with an encouraging vista pulling the walker forward.

Hallsands is two places: the 'new' settlement on the cliff top; and the old ruined village on the rock ledge below **58** (see page 113). This celebrated case of coastal erosion has achieved world-wide fame. The way down to old Hallsands is opposite Trouts Restaurant (comprising restaurant, tea room, ice cream sales and accommodation).

The Coast Path passes in front of Trouts and goes behind the Hallsands Hotel, coming out at Greenstraight, the first of three shingle beaches, each larger than the last, which the walker has to follow.

The Coast Path continues north over Tinsey Head, an easy walk, and Beesands **59** is reached past a thatched cottage at the south end of the village. This linear settlement is now protected by massive boulders, for in the recent past it has suffered, like the villages on either side, from the occasional furious easterly gales.

The path continues north through the caravan site, which conceals Widdicombe Ley to the west. The name defines its use as a provider of withies since Domesday. From Beesands Cellars, at the north end of the beach and an indication of fish

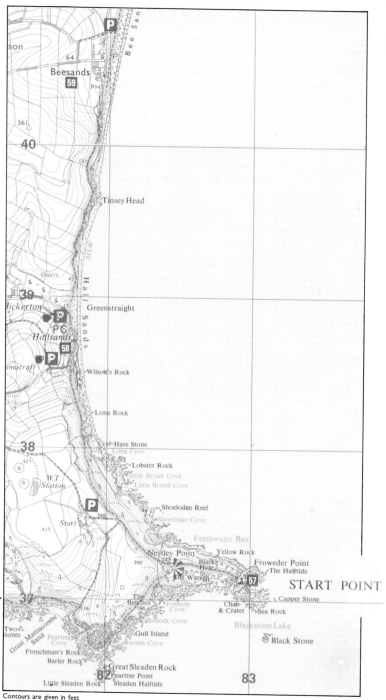

Contours are given in feet
The vertical interval is 25ft

curing in the past, the path goes up behind the house called Sunnydale on the map. (There was also a lime kiln here at one time.) The climb is steep, but not long, and interesting because you get a glimpse of the vast quarry to the right (east) of the path. This is owned by the National Trust, and can be entered from the beach if there is time in the walking schedule. Another possibility, if the tide is low, is to walk along the pebbles to Torcross, but this can be more tiring than slogging up and around the quarry!

Assuming the true Coast Path has been followed, the route descends to Torcross through a tangle of house drives and steps, and there is a choice over the last hundred yards or so. The path comes down – and this should be noted by the east-to-west walker – either by the steps at the south end of the sea wall, or by the public toilets.

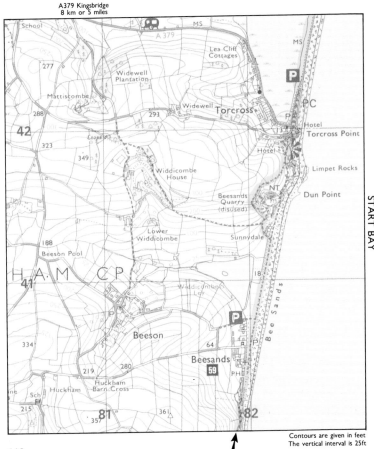

Contours are given in feet
The vertical interval is 25ft

Torcross, with Slapton Ley behind and Slapton Sands in front.

Hallsands

For perhaps three or four hundred years until early this century the houses of Hallsands **58** stood in a row above the beach, secure on their rocky ledge and protected by a shingle foreshore. However, in 1897 the contractor responsible for construction work at Devonport Dockyard was given permission to dredge shingle offshore, from the Skerries Bank. In a very short time 500,000 tons were taken, and the beach level dropped 12 feet (3.7 metres) before dredging stopped in 1902. Its natural defences dissipated, the village was exposed to the sea, and over several years all but one of the 37 houses were wrecked.

Torcross

Torcross is an important place astride the Coast Path. The A379 is met here, there are buses, large car parks, shops, a post office, pubs, restaurants and accommodation. The village is really inseparable from Slapton Ley **60** (see page 127), the stretch of water beside it, but it has been more concerned, historically, with the sea, which nearly demolished the village in 1951 and 1979. The present massive concrete wall dates from 1980.

9 Torcross to Brixham

through Dartmouth and Kingswear
21 miles (34 km)

Beyond Torcross – assuming you are progressing from west to east – the character of the Coast Path changes. For $2\frac{1}{2}$ miles (4 km) the route runs alongside the A379, which is not as bad as it sounds, as the path is off the road.

You are following Slapton Sands, or the Line as it is known locally, which is really shingle, and on the inland side is Slapton Ley **60** (see page 127), although there is nothing to prevent you from following the seaward side if you wish.

After about $1\frac{1}{2}$ miles (2.4 km) a road turns west to the village of Slapton. The parish was recorded at the time of Domesday (1086) and continues to thrive 900 years later. In the village, the dominant building is the 80-foot (24-metre) tower of Sir Guy de Brien's chantry, which he founded in 1372. This was served by four priests whose duty was to ensure that the mass was said for Sir Guy's soul in perpetuity. There is much good building in the village, which has a shop, post office and two inns. The causeway linking the village to the Sands is of fairly recent construction. On the Sands, where the causeway now joins them, there used to be Slapton Cellars, a base for the local fishermen, and a lime kiln. The cellars became the Royal Sands Hotel, but were severely damaged in 1940 when a dog set off some land mines. Invasion practice later in the war completed its demolition.

Just beyond the T-junction a stone memorial **61** marks the use of seven parishes in the Slapton hinterland for invasion practice by the US forces in 1943.

The path continues beside the Higher Ley, now largely silted up, and reaches Strete Gate, where the road veers away from the coast. The gate refers to the time when the Line was used for grazing, and a fence and gate were necessary at the north end to control the animals. Strete Gate Manor House was built here in 1873, becoming the Manor House Hotel in 1937. Six years later it was requisitioned and became a ruin. The site is now a picnic site, and some panels provided by the South Devon Heritage Coast Service explain local features in more detail.

At the north end of Slapton Sands, three-quarters of a mile (1.2 km) beyond Strete Gate, is the site of Undercliffe, another lost village, which probably met its end in 1703. However, from

Contours are given in feet
The vertical interval is 25ft

115

Blackpool Sands.

Strete Gate the path cuts a corner off the A379, but rejoins it one-third of a mile (500 metres) further on.

From here to beyond Stoke Fleming, a distance of over 3 miles (4.8 km), the route of the Coast Path is anything but coastal, touching the coast only briefly at Blackpool Sands. You should not feel conscience-stricken if you take a bus from Strete Gate, at the north end of Slapton Sands, to Stoke Fleming. However, I would urge that the walk round the cliffs at Little Dartmouth is not omitted. Having stated the problems between Strete Gate and Little Dartmouth it should be explained that negotiations to improve this section of the Coast Path are in progress.

The Coast Path now climbs to the A379 at the western end of Strete. This is a busy bit of road, especially in the summer, so walkers must stay in single file, face oncoming traffic, and keep their wits about them. At the first turning left (north), go up Hynetown Road, and follow it round to Strete Church and youth hostel. For a short distance after this point you will be walking on a different route from that waymarked. Apparently the signs were put up incorrectly some time ago. Follow the route description carefully. At the T-junction here, turn right, then left after 100 yards (90 metres), and follow this lane for 300 yards (275 metres) until it emerges on to the A379.

Follow the road around a sharp turn to the right and then take the first turning left at a wall letter-box, back on to the way-marked route. Keep right at the next fork, down a lane that deteriorates to a track after Widewell. At the bottom turn sharp right (east) and the A379 is soon reached at Blackpool Sands.

From where the Coast Path meets the main road it is followed for about 100 yards (90 metres) or so, and the turning north taken by a thatched cottage. This quiet valley-bottom road is followed for a quarter of a mile (400 metres), then turn right (east) up a public bridleway opposite the bridge leading to Blackpool Farm. This is a steep rocky lane called Mill Lane that leads in two-thirds of a mile (1 km) to Stoke Fleming Church.

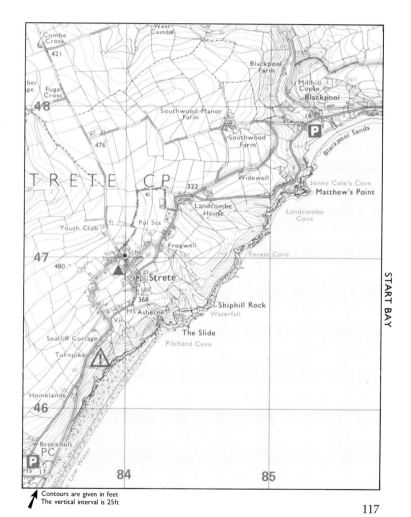

Contours are given in feet
The vertical interval is 25ft

Opposite the church gate turn down Rectory Lane, and enter a footpath at the end by the rectory gate. This brings you to Venn Lane, where you turn right and almost immediately left along Ravensbourne Lane. At the bus shelter turn left and immediately right along a narrow minor road.

Little Dartmouth is reached at a National Trust car park on both sides of the road. Turn right (south) through the newer car park (which was once a tennis court) and follow the path to the coast through a number of gates. Having once more reached the cliffs a fine view unfolds: Start Point to the right, and across the mouth of the Dart to the cliffs east of Kingswear to the left.

The Coast Path now bears east then north, passes round the back of Compass Cove, and dips to sea level at Blackstone Point, crossing a sea-washed gulley by a footbridge. The path climbs gently to meet the minor road at Compass Cottage, with fine views to the right across the mouth of the River Dart.

At Compass Cottage, turn right, but leave the road to walk down through a little park, reaching the road again by the entrance to the National Trust's Gallants Bower property. This is the wooded hill that is such a conspicuous feature in the scene from Dartmouth itself. From the Gallants Bower car park, descend the steps to the lower road above Dartmouth Castle **62**, which can be visited. It was built in the 1480s to defend the town against attack from the sea. The castle is owned and managed by English Heritage. In the summer a boat trip from here can speed one's progress into Dartmouth (see page 129), which is about 1 mile (1.6 km) to the north by road.

In order to cross Dartmouth Harbour refer to page 159. The lower ferry will normally be used, and this delivers you to the

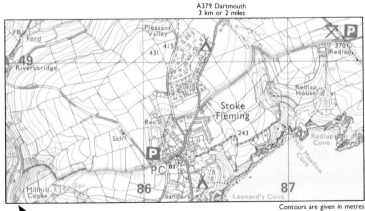

A379 Dartmouth
3 km or 2 miles

Contours are given in metres
The vertical interval is 5m

centre of Kingswear. Although smaller and less important historically than Dartmouth, Kingswear holds on to its railway, the preserved Torbay and Dartmouth Steam Railway, which runs to Paignton at Easter, then from May to early October, on Great Western Railway principles. Kingswear Castle, opposite Dartmouth Castle, has just been bought by the Landmark Trust for conversion into holiday apartments. Maypool Youth Hostel is 3 miles (4.8 km) north of here.

To continue along the Coast Path, pass under the arch by the ferry slip and go up Alma Steps, turning right (east) along Beacon Road. The road narrows to a path and gradually ascends to meet a road where you should continue east, past the small National Trust property of Inverdart.

DARTMOUTH

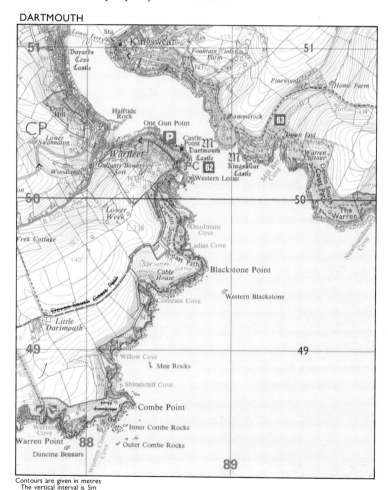

Contours are given in metres
The vertical interval is 5m

After following what is normally a quiet road for half a mile (800 metres) the road turns inland, and 50 yards (45 metres) or so beyond the bend, take a flight of timber steps leading down into the valley. Beside the steps is a memorial plaque **63** to Lt-Col H. Jones, VC, OBE. After his death in the Falklands, it was agreed that a new length of Coast Path, from near Kingswear Castle to Newfoundland Cove, should be opened in his memory; he had strong family associations in the area. Thus it was that this splendid length of path was opened, beginning (or ending) at the ingenious timber steps built by Alan Pope. The memorial was unveiled by 'H' Jones's widow in July 1984.

For the next 6 miles (9.6 km), as far as Sharkham Point, the coast is one of the most beautiful stretches along the entire national trail. Much of it is owned by the National Trust, and there should be no route-finding problems. Link paths head inland to convenient car parks, but it is a strenuous piece of walking.

At the foot of the first descent is Mill Bay, with a small castellated building (marked 'Dangerous'), which used to be a mill. The path climbs steeply up, and enters a Devon Wildlife Trust Nature Reserve.

After about 1½ miles (2.4 km) walking among the Monterey pines, the path levels out, with good views right across Start Bay, and enters National Trust property (the Higher Brownstone on the omega sign refers to a nearby farm) above Newfoundland Cove. Once round the back of the cove the walker is faced with a fork; the lower path is marginally more interesting and rejoins the higher path about 300 yards (275 metres) further on. Now bear right and carry on a short distance to a flat grassy plot with a signpost, surrounded on three sides by Second World War buildings. This was Inner Froward Point Coast Defence Battery **64**. Go to the seat in front of the lookout hut, the one with the steel drop-down shutters: this is a wonderful viewpoint. The island is the Mew Stone. Some buildings are still scattered around among the trees, and there were many more, probably Nissen huts, but all that remain are their concrete bases.

Here is another place where there is a choice of paths heading east. The quick, straightforward route is to leave the grassy plot at the east end, but instead of turning up the steep Military Road, carry on along the signposted path within the woods. After about 300 yards (275 metres) the lower, longer, and more interesting diversion rejoins this higher path from below. The directions for the lower path from the grassy plot are as follows: descend a wartime brick path to the west of the lookout hut, passing two shell magazines, two gun positions and a shell incline, until you almost reach sea level and two searchlight emplacements. The lower path proceeds eastwards, then zigzags up to rejoin the higher path.

Turn right (east) here and after a short distance, in a dip, there is another choice, the high or low path. The higher path leads to a viewpoint on a small eminence, behind Outer Froward Point, from which there is a view inland of the Tower, an 80-foot (24-metre) hollow stone daytime navigational aid built in 1864. The lower path is better for bird watchers.

The two paths come together near a small stream, and the way is now straightforward. Just before Pudcombe Cove a link path from Coleton Farm joins the Coast Path, which now drops steeply into the Coleton Fishacre Valley **65** and up the other side. Access to Coleton Fishacre garden can be gained in the summer on Wednesdays, Fridays and Sundays between 11 a.m. and 6 p.m., and non-Trust members should pay at the main entrance. Coleton Fishacre House was built in 1925–6 by Rupert D'Oyly Carte, son of the Gilbert and Sullivan impresario.

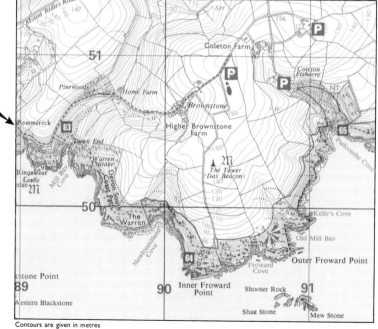

Contours are given in metres
The vertical interval is 5m

Because the Coast Path runs across the grain of the land there is much up and down walking, but a number of link paths make opting out a possibility without trespassing on crops. Between Newfoundland Cove and Sharkham Point there are two small stretches of coast that are not owned by the Trust; they lie between Scabbacombe Head and Scabbacombe Sands, and to the east of Southdown Cliff. Man Sands Cottages are also privately owned.

You leave the wooded area by a squeeze stile and continue a switchback course along the cliffs, aided by waymarks. Above the deep indentation of Ivy Cove another link path heads inland to a car park at Coleton Camp **66**, also a wartime site. The next valley is remarkable for the number of hedges that were removed some years ago, to be replaced by fences, so the area looks like an escaped piece of Dorset downland.

At the next fork in the path take the lower route, unless you are following the National Trust permissive path back to Coleton Camp. This link path follows a line of hedgerows westwards from Scabbacombe Head.

A steep drop down to Scabbacombe Sands – a delightful cove for a bathe – is followed by another uphill slog alongside Long Sands. (Yet another link path goes inland to a National Trust car park in Scabbacombe Lane.) After this a fine free-wheeling stretch brings you down to Man Sands. Two rough approaches (four if you count the Coast Path), its proximity to Brixham and a row of coastguard cottages converted to holiday use make this beach more popular than Scabbacombe Sands. Both are of shingle, and neither has any 'facilities'. There is an old lime kiln at Man Sands. The beach back was repaired with gabions by the National Trust in 1987.

The climb up Southdown Cliff is perhaps the worst of the ascents on this coast, but a level stretch followed by a steep descent makes the walker feel better, and the amble out to Sharkham Point is a Sunday afternoon stroll in comparison. This much-visited headland is a geological curiosity, with a complex of rock types in a small area.

Sharkham Point has survived because it is mostly made of hard rocks. St Mary's Bay, once called Mudstone Bay, backs up against slatey material, which is less resistant. As one looks north from Sharkham Point the change in scenery is very evident. The South Devon holiday area is near at hand, and from here onwards, with a break between Torquay and Shaldon, the trappings of tourism are never far away.

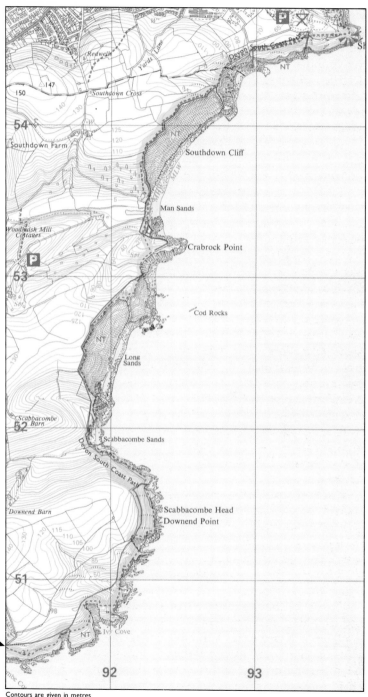

Redwell

Yards Lane

Devon South Coast Path

NT

Sh

147

150

Southdown Cross

54

Southdown Farm

Southdown Cliff

Man Sands

Woodhuish Mill
Cottages

P

53

Crabrock Point

Cod Rocks

NT

Long
Sands

Scabbacombe
Barn

52

Scabbacombe Sands

Devon South Coast Path

Downend Barn

Scabbacombe Head
Downend Point

51

NT

Ivy Cove

92

93

Contours are given in metres
The vertical interval is 5m

123

From the northern base of Sharkham Point the Coast Path goes down a tarmac road, then up left to follow the back of the bay round. Durl Head is the next landmark, a small promontory that gives a rewarding feeling of exposure if you have a head for heights and venture out on to its rocky ridge; but do take care.

Berry Head is getting nearer, and the approach across the common and in through the main gate is recommended. The whole area is now a country park and there is a great deal to see. It is difficult to know where to start, and on a fine day the walker should be prepared to spend an hour or two looking around – at the view, and at the objects of interest near at hand.

The cliffs give good nesting sites for sea birds. Kittiwakes are the noisiest; fulmars have the most attractive flight; guillemots, razorbills, shags and various kinds of gull are also present, so binoculars are useful.

The name Berry is a corruption of the Saxon word *Byri* or *Byrig*, meaning castle or fortification, and until the Napoleonic War fort was built, an Iron Age earthwork and ditch could be seen across the neck of the headland. (Even earlier remains were found in a cave on the approach from Brixham. This is not open to the public.) Unfortunately, when the fort was built the engineer in charge scraped the western approach clean to give a good field of fire, so it is unlikely that much remains to be discovered.

An orientation table at the tip of Berry Head states that Portland Bill is 42 miles (67.5 km) away. Near this useful device is Berry Head Lighthouse, the shortest in the Trinity House service but, after all, it is 190 feet (58 metres) above sea level. Worth seeking out behind the coastguard lookout is the old sentry box, in as good repair now as when it was built. Over the wall from the sentry box is the disused Berry Head limestone quarry. Work ceased here in 1969.

Refreshments are served in the old guardroom, and beside the gate is a cloud-level determining device, in effect a vertical searchlight. Modern technology is also found further inland – a science-fiction type structure that is an aircraft navigational beacon.

When you have been to the end and seen everything, return to the main gate and, having passed through, turn right (north-west) along a tarmac track, but where the track passes into the disused quarry, carry on down a gravel path, bearing left and staying on the main path through the woodland. Soon Brixham Breakwater comes into view.

The road is reached by a circular enclosure now used as a car park. This was a wartime fuel storage tank that had its roof removed. The large hotel was built as the hospital for the Berry Head fort garrison, and was later lived in by the Rev. Henry Francis Lyte of 'Abide with me' fame.

Stay on the road, but at the Shoalstone Beach car park turn towards the shore and walk through some gardens past the swimming pool. The road has to be rejoined (for east-to-west walkers, turn down at Ladybeach Stores) and the last bit of walking into Brixham (see page 128) is along the road.

Contours are given in metres
The vertical interval is 5m

A CIRCULAR WALK ROUND THE COAST AT COLETON FISHACRE

3¾ miles (6.1 km)

From the National Trust car park near Higher Brownstone Farm, walk south along the Military Road, past the Tower (see page 121) to the Inner Froward Point Coast Defence Battery **64**. Now walk east along the Coast Path observing the various high or low path options (see page 121), crossing Coleton Fishacre Valley **65**, and going on to use the link path inland from the back of Ivy Cove (which is signposted). Coleton wartime camp **66** is reached – it is now a car park – and the farm track followed to the road at the Coleton Fishacre crossroads. Carry on across the junction and the car park is reached in a quarter of a mile (400 metres).

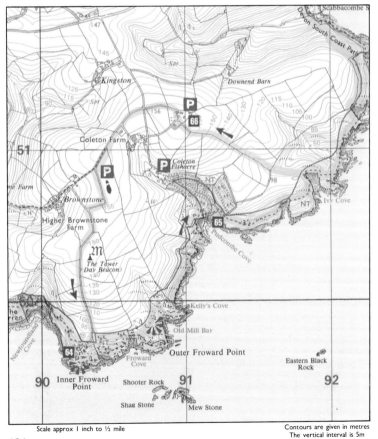

Scale approx 1 inch to ½ mile

Contours are given in metres
The vertical interval is 5m

Water lilies and swans at the nature reserve of Slapton Ley, Devon's largest natural freshwater lake.

Slapton Sands and Ley

The shingle banks of Slapton Sands, Beesands and Greenstraight, and of Chesil Beach in Dorset, originated just after the last Ice Age, when the glaciers melted. Sea levels rose and swept up the material to form the barrier beaches of the present coast. Prior to that the rising land behind the Ley **60** was the coastline.

The line of small concrete posts beside the road was erected to prevent the fragile turf and flora from being damaged by cars. The succession of plants going inland from the sea-washed shingle is interesting and much studied. Starting with the yellow horned poppy, which binds the loose material with its long roots, the progression continues with sand couch grass, sea beet, rest harrow, Danish scurvy grass and rock samphire. Several small fenced areas are set aside to observe the effect when human and animal access is denied.

It is difficult to separate the Sands (the cause) from the Ley (the effect). Slapton Ley is the most extensive natural freshwater lake in Devon, and has long been designated a nature reserve; it became a protected area for birds as long ago as 1896. The Field Studies Council established a Field Centre between the Ley and the village, and this is the base for using the reserve as a conservation, educational, research and recreational resource. Many hundreds of students of all ages attend Slapton Ley Field Centre as residents each year, but there are also displays and facilities for the casual visitor, and trails to walk.

The Ley is nowhere more than 9 feet (2.7 metres) deep and is heavily silted. Eels and pike both grow to a large size, and the pike keep the frogs and ducklings in check. Great crested grebe and Cetti's warbler are two of the birds that have recently started to breed here, but the list of resident and migrant species is lengthy.

A cause for concern in recent years has been the eutrophication of the water. The problem is complex, but high nitrate and phosphate run-offs from the agricultural land, coupled with evaporation and low rainfall, lead to algal blooms that de-oxygenate the water, stifling living creatures, particularly fish.

Brixham

Brixham's past has revolved round its fishing activities, which continue to this day. The town claims to be indirectly responsible for establishing Hull and Grimsby as fishing ports on the east coast. From 1780 onwards Brixham boats started fishing off Kent, partly to 'follow the fish' and partly to be near the London market. They then pushed on into the North Sea and claimed to have discovered the fishing grounds there. Their colonising journeys also led to the development of Scarborough and Fleetwood.

Brixham looked very different before about 1800. Like Dartmouth, it has steep hills on all sides, so the inner tidal harbour was filled in for about half a mile (800 metres) – to well past where the Town Hall now stands – to provide flat land. The fine breakwater was started in 1843 and finished in 1916.

The great event in Brixham's history was the landing of the Protestant William of Orange with an army of over 20,000 men on 5th November 1688. He came to oust the Catholic King James from the throne, and the occasion is referred to as the Glorious Revolution. His statue stands on the quay.

Dartmouth

Dartmouth is a deep-water port of great charm and history. In medieval times it was more important in national maritime terms than it is today, although the presence of the Britannia Royal Naval College continues the naval tradition.

The Second and Third Crusades left from Dartmouth – what a chaotic turmoil of people, animals and supplies the port must have witnessed then! Later, trade developed with Spain, Portugal, France and Newfoundland.

When all this was happening, Dartmouth was operating from a very cramped site. To us this gives Dartmouth its potent atmosphere, but merchants and ships' captains needed space, and the steep hills sliding straight into the harbour gave no room to expand. So over hundreds of years Dartmouth has pushed outwards into the estuary. The visitor should realize that all Dartmouth's flat land is in fact made-up land created from the river.

The town is full of fine buildings. The Butterwalk is a Grade 1 listed building, containing the town museum, and St Saviour's Church has a gallery dating from 1633. Bayard's Cove near the Lower Ferry is powerfully evocative of the rollicking days of sail and some of *The Onedin Line* was filmed there.

Smoke from the preserved steam railway across the harbour reminds one that Thomas Newcomen (1663–1729), who produced the first industrial steam engine, was born in Dartmouth. In a building near the Butterwalk is an early 19th century example of a Newcomen engine.

The massive Royal Naval College was built only in 1905, although it has been enlarged since. It replaced several superannuated 'wooden walls' – hulks from the days of sail used as accommodation for naval cadets – moored in the Dart.

Pleasure boats leave from the quay in every direction during the summer, and a trip upriver to Totnes is one of Devon's great experiences. Walkers should not try to reach Brixham by boat, as the walk around the cliffs is very special, but to see the shore from the sea having once walked it is a noble ambition.

129

The boat float, at Dartmouth.

130

131

10 Brixham to Shaldon

taking in Torquay and its harbour
19 miles (30.8 km)

The first part of this walk, as far as Torquay, is another section
the long-distance walker *could* leapfrog and thereby miss only
a near-urban length of the Coast Path. Buses run through
Paignton, but the most pleasant way to reach Torquay is to use
one of the launches that shuttle across Torbay in the summer.

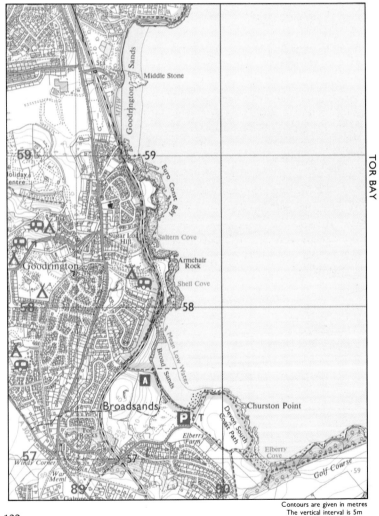

TOR BAY

Contours are given in metres
The vertical interval is 5m

From Brixham Quay **67** (*see map below, continuing on page 132*), walk up Overgang, and along Blackball Lane, then descend to Freshwater Quarry car park. At the far end climb the steps and at a small open area stay up high, and do not be tempted to descend to the first cove, Fishcombe Cove **68**. Carry on above this cove, then the path soon begins to drop to the second cove, Churston Cove, which is crossed above the high-water mark.

There now follows a steep but pleasant climb, which leads to a long, straight, green corridor where the walker is confined both physically and visually; by a fence and Churston golf course on one side, and thick woods on the other. At the western end of this stretch the path zigzags down to Elberry Cove. The small ruined building was the bathing and boating station of the Buller family of Lupton House, 1½ miles (2.4 km) inland. If the sea is calm you may spot a freshwater spring bubbling to the surface off the beach.

Follow the grassy headland of Churston Point round to the aptly named Broad Sands. (A free leaflet describing three circular waymarked walks starting from Broad Sands car park can be picked up from local tourist information centres.) Stay with the sea wall to a point beyond halfway, when you turn away from the beach **A** and head inland along a tarmac track under the railway viaduct. Do not be tempted to ascend the rough land or walk to the far end of the beach.

Having passed beneath the viaduct, turn sharp right up a flight of steps to reach the path beside the railway, then follow it to Goodrington. The railway is, of course, the one you saw earlier at Kingswear. At Goodrington, follow the promenade to the north end, passing the enormous new leisure centre called

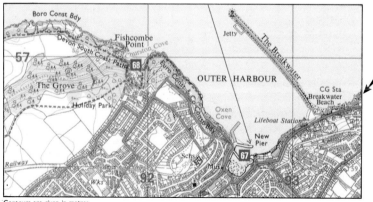

Contours are given in metres
The vertical interval is 5m

Paignton beach and pier.

Quaywest, which will be delighting the visitors to this popular part of Torbay. When faced with Roundham Head, slant up the path through the shrubbery on the steep cliff face, noticing the red conglomerate rock.

The path follows the edge of the pitch-and-putt course, and the route – for it is hardly a path here! – reaches Cliff Road and passes down to Paignton harbour. The architecture of Paignton is undistinguished, but Kirkham House in Kirkham Street is a 14th century building, beautifully restored in 1960.

As well as being the terminus of the steam railway that puffs to Kingswear, Paignton is the end of the BR branch line which serves Torquay from Newton Abbot.

Paignton promenade is now followed to the far end, where a brief diversion inland **B** has to be made round some hotels to reach Preston Sands to the north. If the tide is low, the beach can be used.

At the north end of Preston Sands walk up the road leading to Hollicombe Head, and at the end of the open ground, instead of turning left to the main road, take the path down to the beach and emerge below the railway into Hollicombe Gardens, where the gas works used to be. This little park was opened in 1979.

Having reached the main road, the A379, there is a pavement all the way to Torquay harbour, about 1½ miles (2.4 km), or a bus could be taken. The open-top buses are fun to use on a fine day. Once past Corbyn's Head the character of Torbay changes, and the elegance one associates with Torquay takes over.

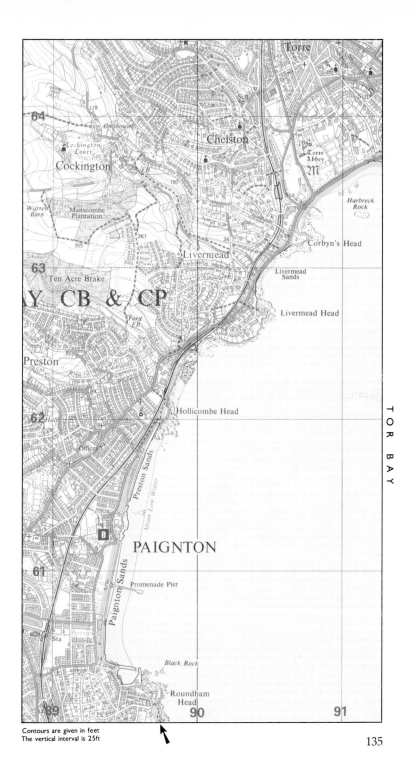

TORBAY

From the south-east corner of Torquay harbour walk up Beacon Hill, and turn in as if you are going to the Imperial Hotel, Torquay's five-star hotel. Walk up the sloping drive in front of the main entrance and follow this path to the end, where there is a view of the curiously named limestone feature, London Bridge, a rock arch. Climb the steps 15 yards (14 metres) from the end of the path. These are steep and lead to Rock End gardens through which you thread your way, passing a gazebo, and finally emerging on Daddyhole Plain through an arch at the southern corner.

Leave Daddyhole Plain by steps at the east end and follow a tarmac path down. A short alternative can be taken through the trees keeping close to the cliff edge, and this will bring the walker back to the tarmac path.

Enter the path on the right signposted 'car park Meadfoot Beach', descend the steps, and meet the road at the west end of Meadfoot Beach. The impressive Hesketh Crescent (1846) on the left as you descend is now the Osborne Hotel although part is let as timeshare apartments.

At the east end of the beach go up the signposted path from a small car park; this cuts a corner beneath Kilmorie flats. Follow the road up, facing oncoming traffic. You are on the Marine Drive, opened in 1924. Notice the evergreen holm oaks, which are such a feature here, and as the road opens out, take the

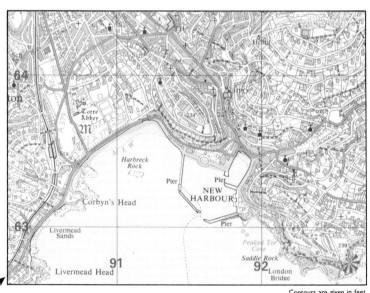

Contours are given in feet
The vertical interval is 25ft

signposted path right. This passes round Thatcher Point through a well-manicured public open space called Hillway Close, given anonymously to the local authority in 1968, and then returns to the Marine Drive; 250 yards (230 metres) further on a turning right to Hope's Nose is an optional extra. This path is opposite Thatcher Avenue. Hope's Nose is a low-level promontory that people have done their best to make even smaller. In the 19th century it was extensively quarried and ships came right into the point to be loaded with the limestone. Now it is frequented mostly by sea anglers.

Back on the Marine Drive, follow the footpath north beside the higher side of the road. There are views ahead of red rocks. At a seat, descend some steps, walk 100 yards (90 metres) down the road, and enter a path on the right by a modern white house called 'Hope Cove House' C. There is a signpost a short way into the path marked 'Bishop's Path'. Go along here, turn right at a tarmac drive, and follow the obvious path round. Although this is the preferable route, the official path follows the road to the left at the white house C. After 175 yards (160 metres) you take a path on the right to meet the tarmac drive on the left.

After the path has gone round Black Head an optional, lower path loops down through the woods and rejoins the main path 300 yards (275 metres) or so further on. There is little to gain from using it.

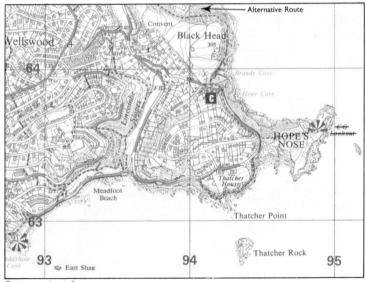

Contours are given in feet
The vertical interval is 25ft

Oddicombe cliff railway.

The Coast Path now reaches the large car park above Anstey's Cove and Redgate Beach, where there are the usual facilities. In summer an occasional boat service runs to Torquay harbour. The two beaches are linked by a raised walkway round the cliffs, and there is a steep route up from the north end of Redgate Beach linking with the Coast Path, which eliminates the need to return up the Anstey's Cove road. The jagged outline of Long Quarry Point is worth noting from Anstey's Cove. This beach is a designated Eurobeach.

Carrying on from the top of the Anstey's Cove road, turn right (north) and 100 yards (90 metres) further on turn right again up some steps signposted 'Coast Path', and then right at a fork. The path emerges on to Walls Hill or Babbacombe Downs, and the fence should be followed round. Once over the top a good view opens up ahead. All the cliffs are red from Oddicombe Beach onwards, except at Petit Tor Point, where a massive limestone 'ice cream scoop' has been quarried out of the cliff. This is known as the Giant's Armchair.

The clifftop hedge should be followed until you see a well-worn path heading into the scrub. Go down here. It descends steeply to a minor road. Turn right, then take the path signposted 'Babbacombe Beach'. Turn right again before a stone arch, and the path zigzags down many steps to emerge above the beach by the red-tiled Cary Arms **69**. This is Babbacombe. Until Torquay developed as a holiday resort Babbacombe was a small fishing village. The pier was built in 1889.

Walk along behind Babbacombe Beach, round the corner of a rock face held in place with motorway netting and rock bolts, and along the newish sea defences to Oddicombe Beach. This is also a designated Eurobeach, reached from Babbacombe by a cliff railway of the kind also found at Lynmouth and Hastings. This one was opened in 1926, carries 40 passengers, and averages about 654 miles (1,052 km) each season!

To walk the Coast Path onwards from Oddicombe Beach you have to climb up the zigzag road, used for occasional hill-climb competitions and at the second bend enter a path on the right beside the cliff railway. You pass beneath the railway, then up and down, carrying on along the coast by descending through sycamore woods into a deep, peaceful, grassy valley. Now follows a steep climb, using railway sleepers as steps, to an open viewing area with several seats.

The Coast Path is now briefly channelled between a fence guarding a cliff edge to the east and a wall on the west protecting private houses. Then the path reaches a well-mown public open space with seats. Ahead is the rocky crag of Petit Tor with a trig

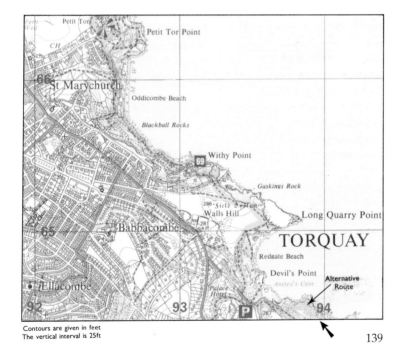

Contours are given in feet
The vertical interval is 25ft

point on its summit. If time allows, a stroll down the grassy tongue towards the sea adds a new perspective. Turn south at the bottom, and if the tide permits one can gain access to the north end of Oddicombe Beach from here, and there is a chance to bathe off the rocks, a conglomerate sandstone containing pebbles, like currants in a bun. If not, turn north from the foot of the grassy slope and you can reach Petit Tor Beach, favoured by naturists and sea anglers.

Back at the top, carry on north to the right of a typical Torquay Italianate house. Petit Tor can be climbed, but the Coast Path passes to the west. Petit Tor marble enjoyed a vogue in the 18th and 19th centuries, but has passed out of fashion.

The golf course is over the fence on the left, and the way is clear along a wide path showing evidence of badgers, rabbits and moles. At a three-path junction take the right-hand one, and a short distance further on fork right again. Now stay on the main path which contours north. (A lower loop path leaves this one to rejoin it further on.) At a small valley, faced with a choice, go right, and carry on round a long left-hand bend down to the valley road at Watcombe **70**. You may want to consider a detour to Watcombe Park, the estate landscaped by Isambard Kingdom Brunel, who planned his country home there.

Having reached the valley road leading to Watcombe Beach **70**, turn left for 20 yards (18 metres), then right, and climb to the Valley of Rocks. In the bowl, turn right and at a fork bear left, and the path now goes for 50 yards (45 metres) along a ledge hacked out of the cliff. Railings on the inside give security, but anyone lacking a head for heights may have problems here. This is the Goat Path **71**.

The Coast Path reaches a lane, which it now follows briefly. Nowhere else between Torquay and Shaldon is the walker so far from the sea – all of 300 yards (275 metres)! However, at the top of a rise take a stile on the right, which brings you down a lane, then to a fenced-off path that leads along several field edges to Maidencombe. This is the last opportunity for refreshment before the tiring 3½-mile (5.6-km) switchback cliff-edge path to Shaldon.

Leave Maidencombe by the road going north from the car park entrance, bearing left behind the last house. The route is straightforward now, and just when one is getting jaded with the ups and downs, the Coast Path meets the A379, enters the top field above Shaldon and begins to free-wheel down past the pitch-and-putt course, with encouraging views ahead.

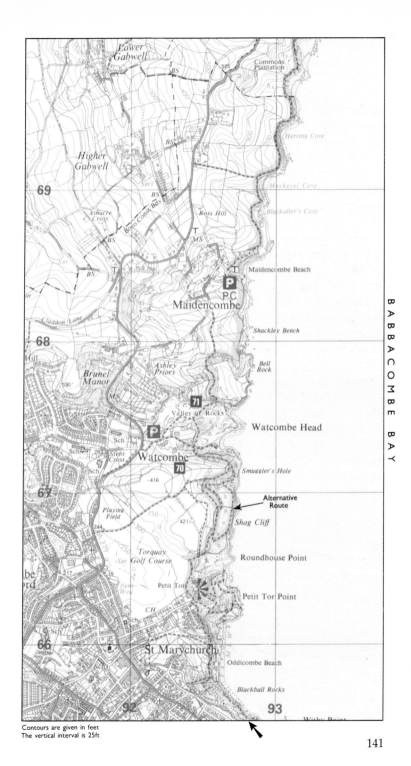

Contours are given in feet
The vertical interval is 25ft

Soon after passing into the second pitch-and-putt field, enter a hedge gap on the right, go down some steps and take the gently curving track going down into a deep cutting. When it reaches the pitch-and-putt car park, carry straight on into the trees. The path leads to the top of the Ness, such a feature in the South Devon landscape. Old prints show the Ness bare of trees; the present grove was planted to mark Queen Victoria's coronation. At the top, turn left and descend to Shaldon, from where the ferry leaves for Teignmouth. (If walking from east to west, leave Shaldon by climbing the Ness, leaving all buildings on your right.)

Between Shaldon and Teignmouth is the shingle bank called the Salty, a firm expanse where fishermen dig for bait between the tides. Beneath the Ness a well-lit pedestrian tunnel probes to a sandy cove known as Ness Beach. This is another designated Eurobeach.

The present bridge dates from 1931, and a toll was collected at the north end until 1948. The walker can reach Teignmouth (see page 152) by the bridge if the ferry is not running (see page 160).

Shaldon Beach with the Ness beyond.

A381 Bishopsteignton
1 km or ½ mile

74
Coombe Lane
Higher Coombe Farm
Coombe
82
The Lee
Sch
Broadmeadow
Hospl

Teignmouth & Shaldon Bridge
Old Quay
New Quay
The Salty
Pier

Gravel Point
Sch
Ferry
F
The Point
Mean High Water
Mean Low Water

31
Shaldon
72
Long Lane
The Ness Hotel
P
Euro Const & Co Const Bdy
E

Ringmore
Commons Lane
Ness Cove
Moorlands
Rushlands
88
SHALDON CP
BS MS
96
Bundle Head
Elmira
New Barn Farm
Butterfly Lane
149
South Devon Coast Path

71
BS
The Beacon
169
Smugglers Cove
NTEIGNHEAD CP
Labrador Bay
Millen Lane
Dean Cottage
Dean Lane
nteignhead
Teignmouth Road
P
137
BS
92
93
MS
94
South Devon Coast Path
MLW
R

Contours are given in metres
The vertical interval is 5m

143

BABBACOMBE BAY

The growth of the South Devon holiday area

The earliest holiday 'resorts' in South Devon were Exmouth and Teignmouth. Dawlish quickly followed, and had a bath house and public rooms by 1812. These three places were handy to Exeter, which at the beginning of the 19th century was a provincial centre of some importance.

The story of Torquay's growth is more complicated, and bedevilled by a kind of mythology which attributed the development of the town to the presence in Torbay of the Channel Fleet during the Napoleonic Wars. The officers are supposed to have lodged their families in the embryo resort.

However, Percy Russell, writing in his scholarly book *A History of Torquay and the Famous Anchorage of Torbay* (1960) found no evidence for this theory, and was firmly of the view that the medical officers on duty with the Fleet understood the climatic benefits of the sheltered site of Torquay and recommended it to their consumptive patients. There can be no doubt that it was as a haven for invalids that Torquay's reputation was made.

Of course, the Napoleonic Wars had closed the Continent to English travellers, and those who had done the Grand Tour saw similarities between the Mediterranean and Torbay. Add to these ingredients the fact that the Palk and Cary families owned much land round Torquay and were ready to sell (at the right price), and we have the makings of Torquay as a fashionable watering place. The final fillip was the kudos provided by a visit from royalty, and in 1833 Princess Victoria came to Torquay with her mother.

Ruskin christened Torquay the 'Italy of England' and Italianate residences, with names such as Villa Borghese and Villa Como, sprang up. Napoleon Bonaparte had been brought to Torbay en route to St Helena in 1815 and even he said the scenery reminded him of Porto Ferraio in Elba.

The railway arrived at Torre, Torquay, in 1848, and from then on the population increased rapidly. It took eleven years to push the line on to Paignton, which then became the popular resort on the bay. It had better beaches and a flatter topography. Brixham was a late starter in the holiday stakes, and until the late 1940s was the olde-worlde fishing village that people visited while staying in Torquay or Paignton. But as land was used up elsewhere, post-war development of the chalet kind squeezed into the higher parts of Brixham, and that is what the west-to-east walker sees first.

Dawlish Warren from Langstone Rock, with the Exe Estuary beyond.

Torquay

The rise of Torquay to become Devon's largest holiday resort
has just been told briefly. If this gives the impression that the
town is a latter-day upstart, it should be pointed out that
evidence of human occupation dating back to between 20,000
and 30,000 BC was found when Kent's Cavern was excavated.
This cave is situated in that part of Torquay between Meadfoot
Beach and Anstey's Cove, and is open to the public.

From about 1200 until the Dissolution of the monasteries
Torre Abbey flourished behind what we now know as Torre
Abbey Sands. The tithe barn survives and some of the original
buildings have been incorporated into what is now, after many
vicissitudes, the borough's art gallery and museum. The little
room devoted to Agatha Christie – who was born in Torquay,
and lived for many years on the River Dart – is alone worth
deviating from the Coast Path to see.

The Coast Path walker is likely to pass the Pavilion, where the
Princess Gardens meet the harbour. This singular structure, so
elegant and redolent of Torquay's artistic past, is now enjoying
a revival as a shopping mall. It was built in 1911 as a concert hall,
and famous conductors performed here – Beecham, Boult,
Wood and Barbirolli – and Elgar also made a guest appearance.

11 Teignmouth to the Exe

via Dawlish and Starcross
11¾ miles (19 km)

From Teignmouth there is the possibility of taking a bus east-wards, to Dawlish, Dawlish Warren or Starcross; the choice is yours. On this next section of the Coast Path the walker is closer to the sea for longer stretches than anywhere else, but there is at first an urban feel about it which I can assure you is only temporary. The route – assuming a low tide – is as follows.

Teignmouth promenade leads to the limestone sea wall which protects the railway from the waves. The railway is the main line between Paddington and Penzance, one of Isambard Kingdom Brunel's great civil engineering achievements.

The distance from the ferry to the end of the sea wall is very nearly 2 miles (3.2 km), and as you leave the sound of the sea to climb up Smugglers Lane **A** you see one of the five tunnels Brunel had to build to bring the railway round the coast.

Should the tide be high or getting high, then this route, where the path has to go below the railway, is impassable, and considerable time will be spent in backtracking and taking the inland route. This rejoins the Coast Path via the A379.

The route now is up Smugglers Lane **A** to the A379, which is reached opposite a phone box. Turn right (north) and walk up this busy road for 150 yards (135 metres). It may be best to cross to the pavement on the far side, but you will have to re-cross to turn into Derncleugh Gardens. Immediately, go up Windward Lane, and climb the stile on your left after a few yards. This is a fairly recently opened length of path that is fenced in from the fields, but much better than following the road. The path drops steeply almost to the railway, and climbs up the other side of the valley until a waymark and fingerpost direct the walker inland along a contouring path to a flight of steps and a stile between some old farm buildings. You are thus brought out on to the main road once again, this time opposite South Down Road.

Ignore the new road and stay on Old Teignmouth Road past a toll house, but then the old road peters out and you emerge on the new road once again opposite a bus stop. Stay on the east side of the road, and 20 yards (18 metres) over the top of the hill turn right into a small sitting-out area and a little park. Follow the cliff edge down past two lookouts converted into seat shelters, then down a zigzag path to Dawlish boat cove **72**.

Contours are given in metres
The vertical interval is 5m

Dawlish remains a pleasant family holiday resort, and is famous for the black swans that paddle around in the Dawlish Water (the Brook).

Heading east from Dawlish you are once again on the sea wall, and a similar warning to that given at Teignmouth applies here: there is a 300-yard (275-metre) stretch of sea wall, just east of Dawlish Station, which is impassable at high tide. Notices at Dawlish Station underpass and at Langstone Rock (to the east) warn of the danger of attempting this stretch at high tide.

If the tide is low there are no problems and Dawlish Warren Station, $1\frac{3}{4}$ miles (2.8 km) from Dawlish Station, can be reached very easily. If the tide is high you will have to follow the Exeter road out of Dawlish and, where it bears inland **B**, a footpath sign near the Rockstone Hotel shows the way to go. This path runs parallel to the railway and just above it. The sea wall and the inland path meet just south of Dawlish Warren Station – those walking the sea wall path should cross to the west side of the railway by the footbridge – and go past a caravan site to the roundabout in the middle of the Dawlish Warren built-up area.

The sandstone cliffs to the west of Dawlish.

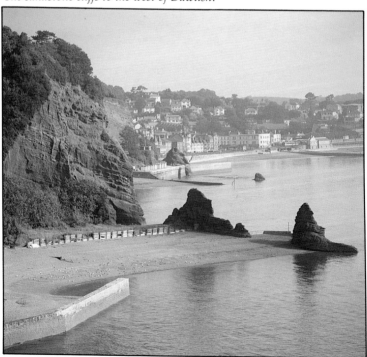

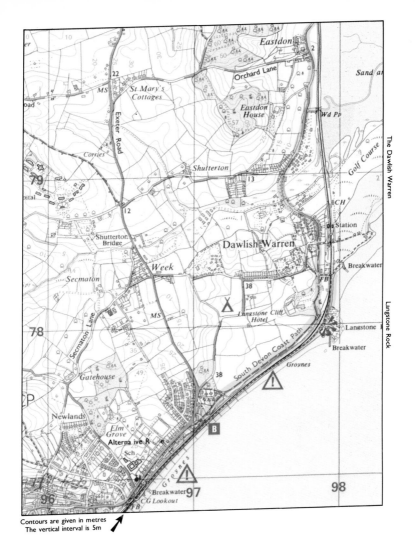

Contours are given in metres
The vertical interval is 5m

Dawlish Warren is a popular resort specialising in chalet, caravan and camping holidays for families. The extensive beach is a designated Eurobeach. A walk out to the end of the Warren itself, the sand bar across the mouth of the Exe, takes one away from humanity to possibly the best bird-watching site along this stretch of the Coast Path. The area is a nature reserve, and part is a golf course. At the far end of the golf course is a two-storey bird hide, which is open to the public. Vast numbers of birds can be seen, and flocks of 20,000 at a time are not unusual. Orchids are abundant, and the tree lupin is a local curiosity.

Powderham Church.

To reach Starcross there is no alternative (except a bus) to a walk along what can be a busy road past Cockwood, where some pleasant pubs provide opportunities for refreshment. At Starcross there is a chance to take a ferry to Exmouth (see page 160), but first a visit to the Brunel Atmospheric Railway Museum **73** (see page 154) in the old pumping house is strongly recommended.

If you intend to cross the Exe at Topsham, carry on up the estuary. From Starcross car park, north of the station, head north to join the minor road following the railway beside Powderham Park. This is a fairly busy road, and there are no views over the estuary for the pedestrian, but for 1 mile (1.6 km) Powderham Park is on the west of the road. Look out here for the herd of fallow deer, and glimpses of Powderham Castle through the ancient oaks. Powderham Castle has been the home of the Courtenay family, the Earls of Devon, since 1390, although the building is a hotch-potch of later building periods. There is a heronry at Powderham.

Where the road turns 90 degrees left (west) the route of the Coast Path continues straight ahead beside the railway. A short digression to view Powderham Church and the fine avenue of evergreen oaks will not add a great deal of time.

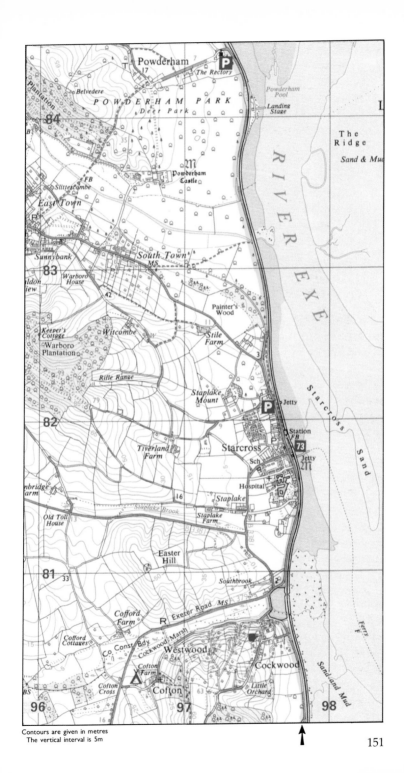

Contours are given in metres
The vertical interval is 5m

151

The path crosses the railway by a level crossing where great care is needed, as the high-speed trains seem to approach quite silently, and carries on north along Powderham Bank. A plaque states that the present sea wall was built in 1963. The outlet of Exeter Canal is reached at Turf Lock, where there is a pub. From this point the canal, with the oldest pound lock in England, built in 1564–66, stretches 5½ miles (8.8 km) to Exeter.

From Turf, where there are usually boats moored, the best way forward is up the west towpath to the bridge over the canal at Topsham Lock. There is a public right of way along the east bank, but from spring to about August the vegetation is allowed to grow. This encourages people to walk up the other towpath, so avoiding disturbance to the breeding birds along this side of the estuary. About 1½ miles (2.4 km) north of Turf you reach the bridge giving access to the east side of the canal. From here a small ferry crosses the River Exe to Topsham at the times advertised (see page 160).

Exeter Youth Hostel is at Countess Wear, on the outskirts of the city, about 2 miles (3.2 km) north-west of Topsham Lock.

You do not have to cross the river here. The towpath can be traced right up to Exeter, and Exeter City Council is creating a Riverside Valley Park that will improve access and confirm the link between the coast and the city. But, however much I may procrastinate, that is the end of the Coast Path from Falmouth to Exmouth. The next section of the South West Coast Path, *Exmouth to Poole*, is covered by Roland Tarr in guide number 11 in the National Trail Guide series.

Teignmouth

Teignmouth is Devon's second oldest holiday resort (after Exmouth), but it had a considerable history before it added summer visitors to its other businesses. A fishing industry was there from early times, and trade with Newfoundland developed in the 18th century. It also exported ball clay, granite and timber, and ships were built on the banks of the Teign. The continuity of its trade is remarkable, for while only a small amount of fishing is now done, Teignmouth is the main exporting port for the ball clay that is mined near Newton Abbot and north of Okehampton. So, on to the coarse industrial base was grafted the elegance that late 18th century visitors expected. Modern recreational activities such as sailing, wind-surfing and sea-angling have now broken the barriers somewhat and take place cheek-by-jowl with the ball-clay ships.

Exeter
4 km or 2½ miles

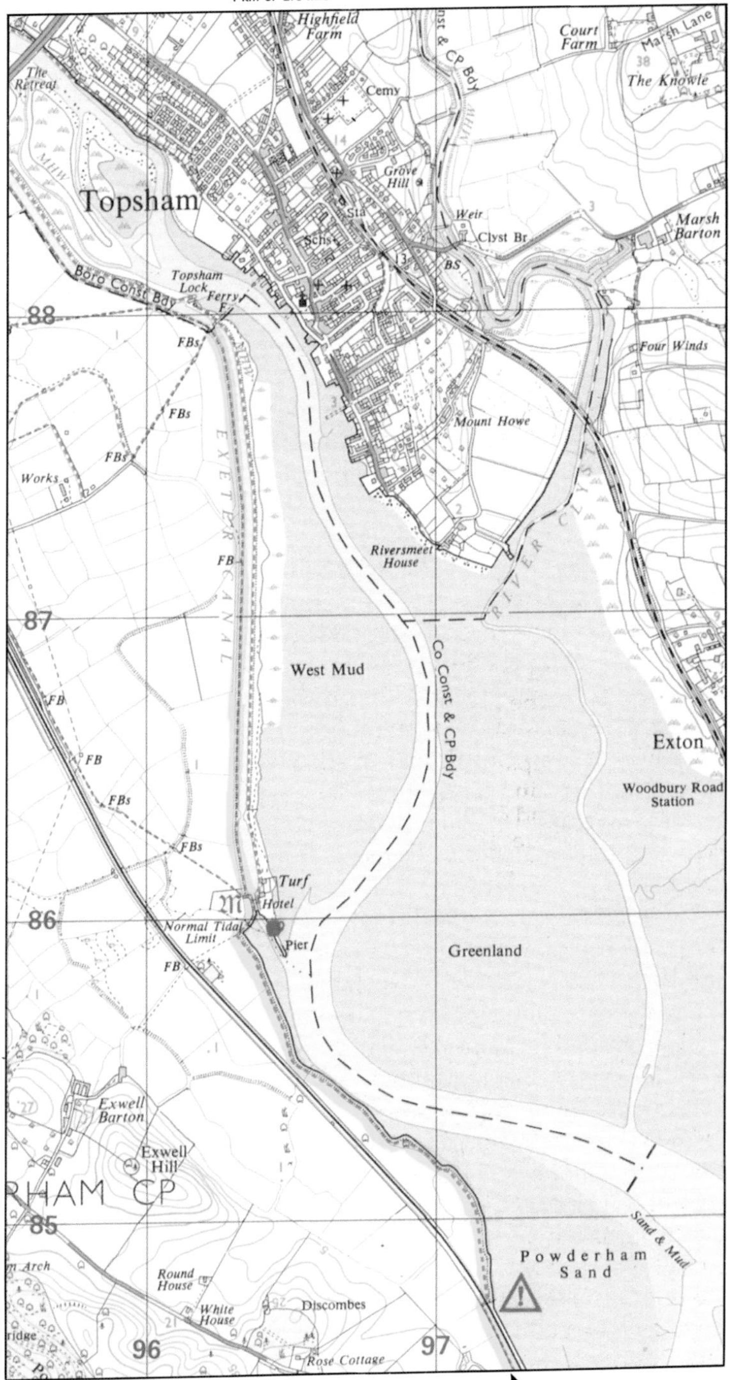

Highfield
Farm

Court
Farm

Marsh Lane

The Knowle

The
Retreat

Cemy

Grove
Hill

Topsham

Sta

Weir

Marsh
Barton

Clyst Br

BS

Topsham
Lock Ferry

Boro Const Bdy

FBs

Four Winds

FBs

FBs

Mount Howe

Works

FB

Riversmeet
House

West Mud

Co Const & CP Bdy

Exton

FB

FB

Woodbury Road
Station

FBs

FBs

Turf
Hotel

Normal Tidal
Limit

Pier

Greenland

FB

Exwell
Barton

Exwell
Hill

RHAM CP

Powderham
Sand

Arch

Round
House

White
House

Discombes

Rose Cottage

EXETER CANAL

RIVER CLYST

Sand & Mud

96

97

Contours are given in metres
The vertical interval is 5m

153

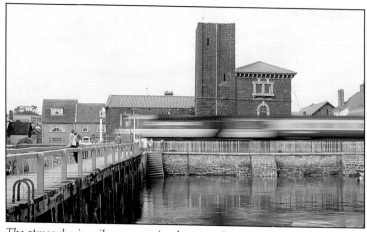

The atmospheric railway pumping house at Starcross.

Brunel's 'atmospheric railway'

Brunel decided to power his trains along this part of the railway on 'atmospheric' principles. A continuous pipe with a longitudinal slot along the top was laid between the rails, and in this pipe ran a piston fitted to the leading vehicle in the train. Stationary steam engines in pumping houses – and Starcross is the last surviving one to have actually worked – pumped out the air in front of the piston, thus forming a vacuum, while air coming in naturally behind the piston pushed the train forward.

In theory the idea was brilliant. It was clean, and when it worked the trains ran speedily and quietly, but Brunel did not have the materials to match the concept. The longitudinal slit along the top of the pipe was sealed with a leather flap valve, and the salt atmosphere and a chemical reaction rapidly rotted the leather. A lubricant was therefore applied to the flap, but this succeeded only in attracting rats and mice, which got sucked into the tube, jamming the pistons and getting blown out into the pumping houses!

The system operated only between Exeter and Teignmouth, and nine trains a day achieved speeds of 70 mph, but so great were the problems that Brunel recommended it be scrapped. A loss of £426,368 was incurred on what became known as the 'atmospheric caper' and conventional locomotives took over.

For years the Starcross pumping house languished. It has now been turned into a well-displayed exhibition **73** about the atmospheric railway, with working models.

PART THREE

USEFUL
INFORMATION

Transport

Rail

Rail services to this stretch of the Coast Path are few and far between. Falmouth, across the Fal from the starting point, can be reached by a branch line from the main line at Truro. Until Plymouth is reached, the only other place on the Coast Path to have a direct rail link is Looe. The branch line for Looe starts on the main line at Liskeard. Plymouth, of course, has frequent trains, but the next places to have full British Rail services are Paignton and Torquay. Teignmouth, Dawlish, Dawlish Warren and Starcross are on the main line, but express trains do not stop at these stations, and the last two have a very sketchy service, although it is better in the summer. Exmouth and Topsham are reached by train from Exeter.

The privately owned Torbay and Dartmouth Steam Railway runs between Paignton and Kingswear (for Dartmouth) at Easter, and then from May to early October.

Buses

The larger centres in Cornwall and Devon, not necessarily on the Coast Path, are served by express coach services from all parts of the country. However, once at places such as Truro, Bodmin, Liskeard, Plymouth and Totnes, it is less easy to find convenient bus links to the coast.

The coastline from Torcross, through Dartmouth to Brixham, Torquay, Teignmouth and Starcross is, however, never far from a main road along which buses run at all seasons. But with bus deregulation it is not always easy to find up-to-date bus times, and *at the time of writing* Cornwall and Devon have slightly different systems operating.

The Cornwall Passenger Transport Unit at County Hall, Truro, publishes a comprehensive public transport timetable every May. The 1988 volume ran to 282 pages and cost 60p plus postage. It is available from local tourist information centres and bus stations. Because some of the services are likely to change during the lifetime of the timetable, an amendment supplement is published free. For example, the 1988 supplement giving details of changes between April and October extended to 56 pages. The office will answer enquiries over the telephone. For further details contact the Passenger Transport Unit, Cornwall County Council, County Hall, Truro, TR1 3BJ. Tel. Truro (0872) 74282.

In Devon there is no comprehensive timetable published *at the time of writing*. However, the Transport Co-ordination Centre at County Hall, Exeter, produces a pile of leaflet time-tables which they can send to enquirers who write or phone, and of course visitors can enquire locally at tourist information centres or bus stations.

The same office publishes a 139-page volume useful for disabled people called *A Guide to Transport Services in Devon: With particular reference to rural communities, elderly and disabled people* (Devon County Council, 1988). For further details contact the Transport Co-ordination Centre, Devon County Council, County Engineering & Planning Department, Lucombe House, County Hall, Exeter, EX2 4QW. Tel. Exeter (0392) 272070 and 272123 – direct lines.

Ferries and river crossings

For complex geomorphological reasons the south-west penin-sula slopes from north to south. This means that the rivers flowing south are generally longer than those flowing towards the Bristol Channel. Rising sea level following the end of the last glaciation – and still continuing – has flooded valleys, forming rias or drowned river valleys. The combination of longer rivers and rising sea level is the cause of this estuary proliferation.

From Falmouth to Topsham or Exmouth there are 13 water obstacles, and only at Looe and Shaldon are there bridges. The long-distance walker must therefore take account of these diffi-culties and plan the journey accordingly. The addresses and times given overleaf are those which obtain in 1989. They may well change from year to year. In all cases the qualification 'weather permitting' applies. The crossings are described from west to east, and an indication of the other seasonal boat trips available along the coast is also given. The use of any of these would materially shorten the walk. For up-to-date information, refer to the nearest tourist information centre (TIC).

RIVER FAL (CARRICK ROADS)

Contact: St Mawes Ferry Co., 14 Rame Croft, Rame, near Penryn, Cornwall, TR10 9EA. Tel. Stithians (0209) 861020.

Falmouth to St Mawes (leaving from Prince of Wales pier) – summer service, beginning mid-May: weekdays 0830 at regular intervals to 1745. Sundays 1000 at regular intervals to 1745. November to March: weekdays 0830 infrequently to 1600. No Sunday service.

St Mawes to Falmouth – summer service, beginning mid-May: weekdays 0900 at regular intervals to 1745. Sundays 1030 at regular intervals to 1730. November to March: weekdays 1900 infrequently to 1630. No Sunday service.

PERCUIL RIVER   *St Mawes to Place*

It is many years since a regular ferry ran between St Mawes and Place, and it is at least 8 miles (13 km) round by footpaths and road. A taxi could be taken from St Mawes, and the St Mawes Ferry Co. (see previous entry) will take parties of 20 or more to Place – the tide permitting – but they must know in advance. Another alternative is to engage the services of a boatman. Anyone doing the walk from east to west must make plans before reaching Place, as there is no phone there and you are unlikely to find an obliging boatman.

RIVER FOWEY   *Fowey to Polruan*

Contact: Polruan Ferry Co. Ltd, Fowey, Cornwall, PL23 1JD. Tel. Fowey (072 683) 2626. Operates all year round. In rough weather the ferry may leave the Fowey side from the Town Quay, and not from the jetty to the south. Signs should be exhibited.

Summer service: weekdays 0700 continuously to 2300. Sundays 0900 continuously to 2300.

Winter service (October to March): weekdays 0700 continuously to 1900. Sundays 1000 continuously to 1700.

LOOE RIVER   *West Looe to East Looe*

The river can be crossed on foot by the bridge which takes the A387 across the harbour, but in the peak summer season a small ferry shuttles across the mouth of the harbour.

RIVER TAMAR   *Cremyll to Stonehouse*

Contact: Penhellis, Maker Lane, Millbrook, Torpoint, Cornwall, PL10 1EB. Tel. Plymouth (0752) 822105. Operates all year round, seven days a week, at regular intervals.

In the summer a boat ferries people between Sutton Harbour (Plymouth) and Cawsand.

RIVER PLYM   *Plymouth to Turnchapel*

It is many years since a ferry ran between Plymouth and Turnchapel. A taxi could be taken to Turnchapel, but buses run there and this would be the best way to reach the start of the South Devon Coast Path.

RIVER YEALM   *Warren Point to Noss Mayo slip*

Contact: P. J. Carter, Futtocks End, The Green, Newton Ferrers,

Devon, PL8 2AL. Tel. Plymouth (0752) 872189. Operates in July and August only, 1100 to 1300 and 1430 to 1600. Possible extra times in good weather from 0900 to 1900. Shout 'Ferry'.

RIVER ERME   *Mothecombe to Wonwell*

There is no ferry, and the only way to cross is to wade the river one hour each side of low water from slipway to slipway. Take great care when flood water is coming down the Erme or if waves are coming in from the sea. There is no other way to get to the other side short of walking through the lanes to Sequer's Bridge on the A379. Little books of tide tables can be purchased cheaply each year, or a local tourist information centre consulted in advance. *The Western Morning News* publishes *high* tides daily for a selection of places in the West Country.

RIVER AVON   *Cockleridge to Bantham*

Contact: H. Cater, Yorick, West Buckland, Kingsbridge, Devon, TQ7 3AQ. Tel. Kingsbridge (0548) 560593. Operates for two weeks at Easter. End of May to August, Monday to Saturday 1000 to 1100 and 1500 to 1600.

Wading the Avon at low tide is not recommended. To reach Bantham by road necessitates a lengthy diversion through Aveton Gifford.

SALCOMBE HARBOUR   *Salcombe to East Portlemouth*

Contact: The Salcombe Ferry Co. Ltd, The Garden Flat, Springfield, Devon Road, Salcombe, TQ8 8HQ. Tel. Salcombe (054 884) 2863 or 2061. Operates all year round. April to October continuous service until 1930 daily. Saturdays, Sundays and Bank Holidays in July and August starts at 0830. November to March 0800 to 1700, half-hourly service.

In the summer a boat ferries people between Salcombe and South Sands Beach.

RIVER DART   *Dartmouth to Kingswear*

Contact: South Hams District Council, Ferry Manager's Dept, The Square, Kingswear, Dartmouth, TQ6 0AA. Tel. Kingswear (080 425) 342. Lower ferry: runs all year round, seven days a week, 0700 to 2255. Sunday starts 0800. Summer service, every six minutes. Winter service, every twelve minutes.

A passenger ferry also crosses to Kingswear from the Dartmouth boat float, and the higher ferry (vehicle) crosses further up the river. In the summer a boat ferries people between Dartmouth and Dartmouth Castle, and boats also run between Dartmouth and Torbay, and between Dartmouth and Totnes.

TOR BAY   *Brixham to Torquay*

Contact: Western Lady Ferry Service, Dolphin Shipyard, Galmpton, Brixham, TQ5 0EH. Tel. (0803) 842424. In the summer a regular service of comfortable vessels takes passengers across Tor Bay between 1015 and 1800.

A boat service operates between Torquay and Anstey's Cove in high summer. Details from Torquay tourist information centre.

RIVER TEIGN   *Shaldon to Teignmouth*
Contact: Teignbridge District Council (Tourism Dept), Sea Front,
Teignmouth, TQ14 8BE. Tel. Teignmouth (0626) 779770. Operates all
year round, except at weekends between November and Easter. From
Easter to October it usually starts at 0800 but finishes at different times,
depending on the month.

RIVER EXE   *Dawlish Warren to Exmouth*
Contact: Exmouth Water Taxi Service, Mr I. Stuart, 129 Exeter Road,
Exmouth, EX8 1QF. Tel. Exmouth (0395) 279693. The Water Taxi may
be able to collect a walker from the east end of Dawlish Warren if
arranged in advance. End of March to mid-October.

RIVER EXE   *Starcross to Exmouth*
Contact: Mr B. Rackley, Starcross Pier & Ferry Co., 26 Marine Parade,
Dawlish, EX7 9DL. Tel. Dawlish (0626) 862452. Seasonal from
1 May until late October, seven days a week, 1000 then on the hour
until 1745 from Starcross. From Exmouth, 1030 then on the half-hour
until 1815.

RIVER EXE   *Topsham Lock to Topsham*
Contact: Exeter City Council, Leisure & Tourism Dept, Civic Centre,
Exeter, EX1 1JJ. Tel. Exeter (0392) 77888. Operates all year round, six
days a week, not Tuesdays. Closed for lunch 1300 to 1400. May to
September 0800 to 2000. October to April 0800 to 1730.

Accommodation contacts

A list of tourist information centres (TICs) is given below; they
will answer enquiries about accommodation, including camping. It is best to approach the TIC nearest to the place you wish
to stay. Note that not all TICs are open throughout the year.
Most operate (for a fee) a 'book a bed ahead' service for personal
callers for the same or the next night. Finding accommodation in
the peak holiday period is not easy, so booking in advance is
recommended.

Youth hostels and camp sites are noted on the Ordnance
Survey maps in this guide, although the walker will find that
many additional camp sites spring up during the summer. The
solitary backpacker may be able to camp in a farmer's field, but
permission should always be obtained first.

The Ramblers' Association yearbook and South West Way
Association guidebook – both published annually – list bed and
breakfast places (see useful addresses on pages 165 and 166).

Tourist information centres (TICs) – from west to east

* = open in the summer months only

Cornwall

Falmouth TIC, 28 Killigrew Street, Falmouth, TR11 2RT. Tel. Falmouth (0326) 312300.

Fowey TIC, The Ticket Shop, The Post Office, 4 Custom House Hill, Fowey, PL23 1AA. Tel. Fowey (072 683) 3616.

Looe TIC, The Guildhall, Fore Street, East Looe, PL13 1AA. Tel. Looe (050 36) 2072.

Devon

Plymouth TIC, Civic Centre, Royal Parade, Plymouth, PL1 2EW. Tel. Plymouth (0752) 264849/264851.

Plymouth TIC,* 12 The Barbican, Plymouth, PL1 2LS. Tel. Plymouth (0752) 223806.

Salcombe TIC,* Russell Court Studios, Russell Court, Fore Street, Salcombe, TQ8 8BS. Tel. Salcombe (054 884) 3927.

Dartmouth TIC,* 11 Duke Street, Dartmouth, TQ6 9RY. Tel. Dartmouth (080 43) 4224.

Brixham TIC, The Old Market House, The Quay, Brixham, TQ5 8TB. Tel. Brixham (080 45) 2861.

Paignton TIC, The Esplanade, Paignton, TQ4 6BN. Tel. Torquay (0803) 558383.

Torquay TIC, Vaughan Parade, Torquay, TQ1 5EG. Tel. Torquay (0803) 27428.

Teignmouth TIC, The Den, Sea Front, Teignmouth, TQ14 8BE. Tel. Teignmouth (062 67) 79769.

Dawlish TIC, The Lawn, Dawlish, EX7 9AP. Tel. Dawlish (0626) 863589.

Exmouth TIC,* Manor Grounds, Alexandra Terrace, Exmouth, EX8 1NZ. Tel. Exmouth (0395) 263744.

The tourist boards associated with these information centres are:

Cornwall Tourist Board, 59 Lemon Street, Truro, TR1 2SY. Tel. Truro (0872) 74057.

Devon Tourism, Devon County Council, County Hall, Exeter, EX2 4QQ. Tel Exeter (0392) 273260.

West Country Tourist Board, Trinity Court, 37 Southernhay East, Exeter, EX1 1QS. Tel. Exeter (0392) 76351.

Looking west from Tregantle Cliffs, with the rifle range on the right.

Facilities for walkers

Once a place reaches a certain size a walker may expect it to have the facilities of car park, pub and toilets, and towns such as Looe, Dartmouth and Torquay have many of these.

Rather than mask other detail on the maps with a multiplicity of symbols, the towns and villages that fall into this category are listed below. Some are slightly off the path, and others, such as Millendreath and Challaborough which are totally given over to holiday business, may have facilities that are closed out of season.

Cornwall
St Mawes
Portscatho
Gerrans –
    slightly off the
    Coast Path
Portloe
Gorran Haven
Mevagissey
Pentewan
Charlestown
Par
Polkerris
Fowey
Polruan
Polperro
West Looe
East Looe
Millendreath
Downderry

Portwrinkle
Crafthole –
    slightly off the
    Coast Path
Cawsand
Kingsand
Cremyll

Devon
Plymouth
Turnchapel
Wembury
Noss Mayo –
    slightly off the
    Coast Path
Challaborough
Bigbury-on-Sea
Bantham
Outer Hope
Salcombe

East Prawle –
    slightly off the
    Coast Path
Beesands
Torcross
Strete
Stoke Fleming
Dartmouth
Kingswear
Brixham
Paignton
Torquay
Babbacombe
Maidencombe
Shaldon
Teignmouth
Dawlish
Dawlish Warren
Starcross

Useful addresses

The Association of Lightweight Campers, c/o The Camping & Caravanning Club, 11 Lower Grosvenor Place, London, SE1W 0EY. Tel. London (01) 828 1012.

Cornwall Trust for Nature Conservation, Five Acres, Allet, Truro, TR4 9DJ. Tel. Truro (0872) 73939.

Countryside Commission (headquarters), John Dower House, Crescent Place, Cheltenham, Glos, GL50 3RA. Tel. Cheltenham (0242) 521381.

Countryside Commission, South West Regional Office, Bridge House, Sion Place, Clifton, Bristol, BS8 4AS. Tel. Bristol (0272) 739966.

Devon Wildlife Trust, 35 New Bridge Street, Exeter, EX3 4AH. Tel. Exeter (0392) 79244.

Long Distance Walkers' Association, 11 Thorn Bank, Onslow Village, Guildford, Surrey, GU2 5PL. Publishes a handbook available free to members.

Mount Edgcumbe Country Park, Cremyll, Torpoint, Cornwall, PL10 1HZ. Tel. Plymouth (0752) 822236. Publishes theme leaflets on a variety of topics.

National Trust, Cornwall Regional Office, Lanhydrock, Bodmin, PL30 4DE. Tel. Bodmin (0208) 74281. Publishes leaflets about its properties along the coast.

National Trust, Devon Regional Office, Killerton House, Broadclyst, Exeter, EX5 3LE. Tel. Exeter (0392) 881691. Publishes leaflets about its properties along the coast.

Nature Conservancy Council, Regional Office, Roughmoor, Bishop's Hull, Taunton, Somerset, TA1 5AA. Tel. Taunton (0823) 283211.

Ordnance Survey, Romsey Road, Maybush, Southampton, SO9 4DH. Tel. Southampton (0703) 792792.

Ramblers' Association, 1/5 Wandsworth Road, London, SW8 2XX. Tel. London (01) 582 6878. Their annual yearbook has many bed and breakfast addresses. Available free to members; available to non-members from major bookshops and newsagents for £2.95.

Royal Society for the Protection of Birds, South West Regional Office, 10 Richmond Road, Exeter, EX4 4JA. Tel. Exeter (0392) 432691.

South Cornwall Heritage Coast Service, Borough Council Offices, 39 Penwinnick Road, St Austell, PL25 5DR. Tel. St Austell (0726) 65436.

South Devon Heritage Coast Service, Follaton House, Plymouth Road, Totnes, TQ9 5NR. Tel. Totnes (0803) 864499. Publishes a set of nine leaflets about the Coast Path from Brixham to Plymouth.

South West Way Association, Membership Secretary, 1 Orchard Drive, Kingskerswell, Newton Abbot, Devon, TQ12 5DG. Tel. Kingskerswell (080 47) 3061. The South West Way Association exists to help and advise those who enjoy walking this path, and to draw attention to any problems along the route and seek to resolve them. Information to members is by way of an annual guidebook and newsletters.

Youth Hostels Association, South West Area Office, Belmont Place, Devonport Road, Stoke, Plymouth, PL3 4DW. Tel. Plymouth (0752) 562753.

Guided walks

The management and interpretive provision of this stretch of the Coast Path – except on National Trust land, which is looked after by the Trust – is split between the South Cornwall Heritage Coast Service and the South Devon Heritage Coast Service. (Other exceptions are the Coast Path where it passes through Mount Edgcumbe Country Park, and within the Torbay Borough Council boundary.)

Both services organise guided walks conducted by local experts on a wide range of topics, not necessarily in the summer only. They could be general interest walks led by National Trust wardens or local ramblers, or specialist walks, talks, and boat trips, on everything from astronomy to exploring rock pools. There may be a small charge. Leaflets listing these outings can be picked up at information centres, libraries, museums and cafés, or from the offices of the two services (see pages 165 and 166).

Bibliography

Barber, Chips, *The Torbay Book* (Obelisk Publications, 1984).
—— and Chard, Judy, *Burgh Island and Bigbury Bay* (Obelisk Publications, 1988).
Carne, Tony, *Cornwall's Forgotten Corner* (Lodenek Press, 1985).
Clarke, Jennifer, *Exploring the West Country: A Woman's Guide* (Virago, 1987).
Davies, Stan, *Wildlife of the Exe Estuary* (Harbour Books, 1987).
Delderfield, Eric R., *Torbay Story* (Raleigh Press, 1951).

Devon County Council, *Coastlines of Devon* (Devon County Council, 1980).

Dickinson, M. G. (ed.), *A Living from the Sea* (Devon Books, 1987).

du Maurier, Daphne, *Rebecca* (Gollancz, 1938).

—— *The House on the Strand* (Gollancz, 1969; Pan, 1979).

English Heritage, *Register of Parks and Gardens of Special Historic Interest*, Cornwall and Devon entries (English Heritage, 1987).

Fedden, Robin and Joekes, Rosemary, *The National Trust Guide* (Jonathan Cape, 1973/84).

Gardiner, Rena and Trinick, Michael, *A Journey of Discovery: A Guide to some Properties belonging to the National Trust in South Cornwall* (The National Trust, 1987).

Grigson, Geoffrey, *Freedom of the Parish* (Phoenix House, 1954).

Harvey, Phil and Keene, Peter, *Prawle Peninsula Landscape Trail* (Field Studies Council, 1985).

Hoskins, W. G., *Devon* (Collins, 1954).

Hunt, Peter (ed.), *Devon's Age of Elegance* (Devon Books, 1984).

Langley, Martin and Small, Edwina, *Estuary & River Ferries of South West England* (Waine Research Publications, 1984).

—— *Lost Ships of the West Country* (Stanford Maritime, 1988).

Larn, Richard, *The Diver Guide to South Cornwall* (Underwater World Publications, 1983).

—— and Carter, Clive, *Cornish Shipwrecks Vol 1: The South Coast* (David & Charles, 1971).

Le Messurier, Brian, *The Visitor's Guide to Devon* (Moorland Publishing, second edition, 1988).

Luck, Liz, *South Cornish Harbours* (A. & C. Black, 1988).

McDonald, Kendall and Cockbill, Derek, *The Diver Guide to South Devon* (Underwater World Publications, 1982).

The National Trust, *The National Trust in Cornwall: Aerial Views of Properties on the South Coast* (The National Trust, undated).

—— *Properties of the National Trust* (The National Trust, 4th edition, 1988).

Padel, O. J., *A Popular Dictionary of Cornish Place-Names* (Alison Hodge, 1988).

Perkins, John W., *Geology Explained in South and East Devon* (David & Charles, 1971).

Pevsner, Nikolaus (revised by Enid Radcliffe), *The Buildings of England: Cornwall* (Penguin Books, 1983).

—— *The Buildings of England: South Devon* (Penguin Books, 1952).

Pope, Rita Tregellas, *The Visitor's Guide to Cornwall and the Isles of Scilly* (Moorland Publishing, second edition, 1988).

Scott, Anne, *The Good Beach Guide* (Ebury Press, 1988).

Shallcross, Martyn, *Daphne du Maurier Country* (Bossiney Books, 1987).

Soper, Tony, *Wildlife of the Dart Estuary* (Harbour Books, 1982).

—— and Le Messurier, Brian, *The National Trust Guide to the Coast* (Webb & Bower, second impression, 1986).

Weatherhill, Craig, *Cornovia: Ancient Sites of Cornwall and Scilly* (Alison Hodge, 1985).

Wills, Graham (ed.), *Devon Estuaries* (Devon Books, 1985).

Ordnance Survey Maps covering the South West Coast Path (Falmouth to Exmouth)

Landranger Maps (scale: 1:50 000): 192, 200, 201, 202, 204.

Pathfinder Maps (scale: 1:25 000): 1316 (SY29/39)
    1330 (SY08/18), 1342 (SX87/97), 1351 (SX86/96)
    1354 (SX05/15), 1355 (SX25/35), 1356 (SX45/55)
    1358 (SX85/95), 1361 (SW95/SX04), 1362 (SX54/64)
    1363 (SX74/84), 1366 (SW73/83/93), 1367 (SX63/73/83).

Outdoor Leisure Maps (scale 1:25 000): Map 20, South Devon.

Motoring Maps: Reach the South West Coast Path by car using Routemaster Map 8 (scale 1:250 000), 'South West England and South Wales'.

A note to the National Trail Guide user

We hope you like your National Trail Guide.

A great deal of care has been given to accuracy and clarity in compiling these guides but, inevitably, improvements can be made.

To help the publishers in making these books as accurate and useful as possible, your comments and criticisms are welcomed. Please write, giving your own name, address and postcode, and stating which guide(s) you have bought, to the following Freepost address (no stamp required): Countryside Commission, Freepost (GR 1422), Cheltenham, Glos, GL50 3BR.

In return we are offering a new service to you, the user. You will receive a newsletter containing additional information and revisions to help you make the most of the guides and enjoy your walks to the full.